January desolate;
February dripping wet;
March wind ranges;
April changes;
Birds sing in tune
To flowers of May,
And sunny June
Brings longest day;
In scorched July
The storm-clouds fly
Lightning-torn;
August bears corn,
September fruit;
In rough October
Earth must disrobe her;
Stars fall and shoot
In keen November;
And night is long
And cold is strong
In bleak December.

Christina Rossetti

Also available in Piccolo
by Deborah Manley and Peta Rée

PICCOLO BOOK OF GAMES FOR JOURNEYS
PICCOLO BOOK OF PARTIES AND PARTY GAMES

Piccolo
all the year round
book

Deborah Manley

A Piccolo original
Pan Books Ltd London and Sydney

Contents

Acknowledgements

I wish to thank the following for permission to include copyright material:

Faber & Faber Ltd for an extract from *The Country Child* by Alison Uttley; Oxford University Press Ltd for an extract from *Larkrise* by Flora Thompson; Nicky Browne for her article 'Easter Eggs'; and *Punch* for 'The Calendar' by Barbara Euphan Todd.

Prologue

I tell of festivals, and fairs, and plays,
Of merriment, and mirth, and bonfire blaze;
I tell of Christmas mummings, New Year's day,
Of Twelfth Night king and queen, and children's play;
I tell of Valentine's and true-love's knots,
Of omens, cunning men, and drawing lots;
I tell of brooks, of blossoms, birds and bowers,
Of April, May, of June, and July flowers;
I tell of May-poles, hock carts, wassails, wakes,
Of bridegrooms, brides, and of their bridal cakes;
I tell of groves, of twilights, and I sing
The court of Mab, and the fairy king.

Robert Herrick

JANUARY

January brings the snow,
Makes the toes and fingers glow.

The name of the month

January is the door of the new year, named after the Roman god, Janus, the doorkeeper, who is often represented with two faces because he was acquainted with both the past and the future. Replete from the festivities of Christmas and all its excitement, we move into the New Year.

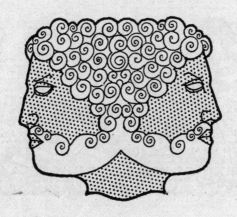

Festivals

New Year's Day. The first day of January is New Year's Day and custom has it that the first 'foot' over the threshold decides the luck of the year. The tradition of who brings good luck varies from place to place. In some parts of the country a dark man bearing a lump of coal brings good luck; in others a fair man carrying a jug of milk. Often, if a woman happens to be the 'first footer', she's thought to bring ill luck. Yet another tradition is that the first 'footer' should come in, bringing in the new year, and then go out again taking something from the house (like a dustpanful of dust) to take the old year out of the house. New Year's Day is now a holiday in all parts of the British Isles, whereas formerly it was a holiday only in Scotland.

Twelfth Night. The twelfth day after Christmas, 6 January, is the Feast of Epiphany, the day on which the three kings, Caspar, Melchior and Balthasar, came to Bethlehem to see the baby Jesus. This is the day when traditionally the last of the Christmas decorations must be taken down. Sometimes people have a party on 5 January, as it is the last night on which the house may be decorated without bringing ill luck.

Down with the rosemary, and so
Down with the bays and mistletoe;
Down with the holly, ivy, all
Wherewith you dressed the Christmas hall,
That so the superstitious find
No one last branch left behind;
For look, how many leaves there be
Neglected, there – maids, trust to me –
So many goblins shall you see.

                                    Robert Herrick

Epiphany also used to be a time when farmers could secure
a blessing for the coming farming year. On the eve of
Epiphany in Devon the farmer and his workers used to take
a cider jug out to the orchard, stand in a circle round the
most fruitful of the trees and drink this toast:

Here's to thee, old apple tree,
When thou may'st bud, and when thou may'st blow!
And whence thou may'st bear apples enow!
Hats full! Caps full!
Bushel, bushel, sacks full!
And my pockets full too!
Huzza!

26 January is Australia Day and India Day, the national
holidays of these two countries.

Weather forecasts

In this book you will find a number of traditional sayings
about the weather – old sayings by country people based on
observations they have made over the centuries. How true
are they, in fact? Collect from this book and other sources
the traditional sayings about the weather and make a
weather chart showing both the traditional forecasts and
what actually happened.

TRADITIONAL FORECASTS FOR JANUARY	JANUARY	ACTUAL JANUARY WEATHER
A FAIR DAY IN WINTER IS MOTHER OF A STORM.	1st	Frosty
IF THE BIRDS BEGIN TO WHISTLE IN JANUARY THERE ARE FROSTS TO COME.	2nd	Very Cold and Frosty
	3rd	Fine day, windy
	4th	Windy and rainy
A JANUARY SPRING IS WORTH NOTHING.	5th	
A SNOW YEAR'S A RICH YEAR.	6th	

Forecasting from the moon

When the moon is pale or has a halo round it there is usually a thin layer of cloud in the sky and this foretells a depression with bad weather on the way. From this comes the old verse:

> If the moon show a silver shield,
> Be not afraid to mow the field;
> But if she rises haloed round,
> Soon we'll tread on deluged ground.

A very white moon shines when the weather is dry, but a very clear outlined moon can indicate strong winds high up which can bring in unsettled weather. So we get the saying: 'The full moon eats clouds.'

Sunrise and sunset

Keep a record of the sunrise and sunset times each day so that you can see how the days gradually lengthen. At the beginning of January the sun rises at approximately 8.00 AM and sets at about 4.00 PM, so we have eight hours of daylight. See how, by the end of the month, we have one more hour of daylight.

Nature notes

January is one of the coldest months of the year. The longest recorded freeze in Britain was in the winter of 1963–4 when in Westmorland the temperature did not rise above 0° centigrade (32° Fahrenheit) for over a month.

Lambing begins in the warmer lowlands of southern England, but the lambs don't begin to be born until February in the Midlands and until March in the north of Britain. When is lambing time in your area?

Things to do outdoors

Feeding the birds

With winter hardening, this is a time when you might like to give some help to the wild birds. It is often hard for them to find enough food and water in the cold. You could make a bird table on your window sill, where you can watch the birds enjoying your offerings from really close range.

Here are two ideas about how to make one:

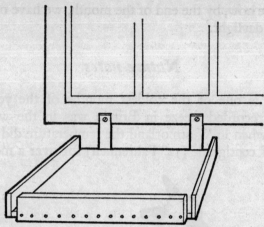

1 Make a tray which will fit on your sill, with a piece of plywood for the bottom and three sides fixed on to it, with gaps between them so that you can clean it off easily. Fix it on to the wooden frame of your window with a metal corner brace. (You might need a grown-up to help with this.)

2 If you would prefer a hanging food tray, make a similar tray with four sides. Fix an arm from the window frame and hang the tray from it with a hook and some wire.

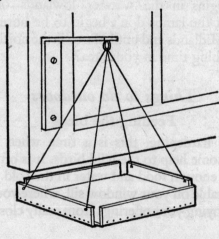

Put out bird seed, peanuts, chopped-up bacon rind (if you don't chop it up, the birds may swallow it whole and choke on it), crusts of bread, and so on. Put out a little bowl of water and make sure it doesn't freeze on icy days.

A visitors' book

Have a small notebook and pencil on the window sill where you can overlook your bird table. Make notes about the different birds who visit your table. How do they eat? What foods do the different birds prefer? Describe their size and markings. You could illustrate these descriptions by drawing and colouring pictures of the birds.

If the birds are migrants, when do they arrive and when do they leave? See if you can find out where they go to in winter. To help you identify birds, you really need a bird book. Here are some suggestions: *Heath and Woodland Birds* by Pemberton (Ladybird); *Collins' Pocket Guide to British Birds* by Fitter and Richardson (Collins); *The Observer's Book of Birds* edited by Benson and Vere (Warne).

A snowman

Have you ever made a snowman? You will need quite a lot of snow before you can make a big one. Start off with a handful of snow which you roll into a rough ball. Now roll

your ball along in the snow so that it builds up into a larger and larger ball, until it is big enough for the body. Then make another slightly smaller ball for the head. Make sure you do not make it too big to lift up on to the body! There is your snowman, though you may want to add more snow to the figure to round it off. Put a scarf round his neck and make features for his face, with stones or bits of coal for his eyes, a carrot for his nose and a stick for his mouth. Borrow a hat to put on his head and perhaps give him a pipe and a stick to carry. As the snow melts, so your snowman will disappear, but there will be a patch of snow where he stood long after all the other snow is gone.

Things to do indoors

What to do with old cards

It seems terrible to throw away old Christmas and other cards – they're so pretty and they cost such a lot too! But unless there's something you want to do with them, they have to go. Here are a few ideas.

Sort through them first to check whether there are any addresses which should be kept or messages which should be answered. Then tear off the plain back sheets and put these in the kitchen drawer to use as shopping lists and notes for the milkman. If some of the backs are made of fairly thick card, you might keep them to use for other things (like patterns for making cut-outs). Now your cards are ready to use.

You can make *gift tags* by cutting the pictures into suitable sizes and pieces of the picture. Making sure there is no

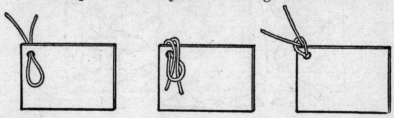

printing or writing on the back, punch a hole in one corner and thread it with wool.

You are likely to have more than you need, so make the spare ones up into cellophane packets of five or ten and store them in a box to give to a Christmas bazaar or a charity shop for sale next November and December for Christmas.

You can use them to make *next year's cards* or *calendars*. Paste pictures from old cards on to folded cards, perhaps adding a few words of greeting or a border of glitter. You can also keep them to use for the pictures in an Advent calendar (*see* page 188).

Some organizations use old Christmas cards for various purposes and advertise for them in the press. The local primary school or children's ward in the hospital may welcome them, too.

Calendars

January is the time to make a calendar for the year ahead.

A one-picture calendar

Get a good piece of strong card of the size you want, a bit of ribbon about 15 centimetres (6 inches) long and a small calendar showing all the months, which you can buy at Woolworth's or a stationer's. You can use one of your own paintings, or a photograph, or you can use a picture from an old Christmas or birthday card to stick on to the

backing card. Make two holes with a punch about 2 centimetres ($\frac{3}{4}$ inch) on either side of the centre of the top of the card and tie the ribbon through the holes, so that the calendar can be hung up. Fix the small calendar at the bottom of the card, below the picture. If your backing card is not big enough for both the picture and the small calendar, take another small piece of ribbon, about 2·5 centimetres (1 inch) long, stick one end firmly to the back of the card at the bottom in the centre and the other end to the back of the small calendar, so that it hangs down below the picture.

A calendar with a picture for each month

Commercial calendars which have a picture for each month of the year usually have a spiral binding to hold them at the top or a perforated edge where you tear off last month's picture. You can't really use either of these methods, so, instead, get two small looseleaf-folder rings from a stationer's to fix the pages of your calendar together at the top, so that the pages can be turned over each month. You will need twelve pieces of light-weight card, which can all be the same colour or can be of different colours; you can buy them from stationers and artshops. The pieces can be any size you want, but must be large enough to take both a picture and a frame containing the days of the month. Collect together or, better still, paint twelve pictures of roughly the same size as each other suitable for the various months of the year. For instance, you could have a snow-scene for January, a seaside scene for August and so on. Try to have something nice and bright for the rather dreary months of November and February when it can be very dull outside. Paste your pictures on to the card, leaving space for the month frames, which can go either below or beside the picture.

Take twelve smallish pieces of white paper the size you want for the calendar itself and print on them the days and dates for each month. You will be wise to copy this from a calendar for the coming year in order to make sure you match the days and the dates correctly! Paste each calendar on to the correct card.

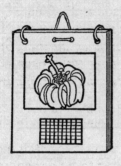

Then punch two holes at the top of the cards, all in the same position about a quarter of the way from each edge. These holes are for the rings. Make two more holes, each 2 centimetres ($\frac{3}{4}$ inch) from the centre of each page, for the hanging ribbon. Fix the pages together with the looseleaf rings and then thread ribbon through the centre holes so that the calendar can be hung.

A year-on-a-page calendar

This is more of a poster, perhaps, than a calendar. It needs very careful planning to get all 365 (or in a Leap Year 366 days) on to one page! You will need a very large piece of paper, too: 60 by 76 centimetres (24 by 30 inches) is about right. Divide the page up into 12 columns down (on our suggested paper size each one would be 5 centimetres [2 inches] deep) and 30 columns across (each one should be 2·5 centimetres [1 inch] across).

In the first square of each row print the name of the month. You will probably have to use the abbreviated form to fit it in, or the initial letter. Then in the remaining 29 columns print the numbers 1 to 27, one to a square, and then use the last two squares for the remaining dates, like this:

A YEAR ON A PAGE CALENDAR																												
JAN.	1	2	3	4	5	6	7	8	9	10	11	12	13	14	15	16	17	18	19	20	21	22	23	24	25	26	27	28/29/30 31
FEB.	1	2	3	4	5	6	7	8	9	10	11	12	13	14	15	16	17	18	19	20	21	22	23	24	25	26	27	28
MAR.	1	2	3	4	5	6	7	8	9	10	11	12	13	14	15	16	17	18	19	20	21	22	23	24	25	26	27	28/29/30 31
APRIL	1	2	3	4	5	6	7	8	9	10	11	12	13	14	15	16	17	18	19	20	21	22	23	24	25	26	27	28/29/30 31
MAY	1	2	3	4	5	6	7	8	9	10	11	12	13	14	15	16	17	18	19	20	21	22	23	24	25	26	27	28/29/30 31
JUNE	1	2	3	4	5	6	7	8	9	10	11	12	13	14	15	16	17	18	19	20	21	22	23	24	25	26	27	28/29/30 31
JULY	1	2	3	4	5	6	7	8	9	10	11	12	13	14	15	16	17	18	19	20	21	22	23	24	25	26	27	28/29/30 31
AUG.	1	2	3	4	5	6	7	8	9	10	11	12	13	14	15	16	17	18	19	20	21	22	23	24	25	26	27	28/29/30 31
SEPT.	1	2	3	4	5	6	7	8	9	10	11	12	13	14	15	16	17	18	19	20	21	22	23	24	25	26	27	28/29/30 31
OCT.	1	2	3	4	5	6	7	8	9	10	11	12	13	14	15	16	17	18	19	20	21	22	23	24	25	26	27	28/29/30 31
NOV.	1	2	3	4	5	6	7	8	9	10	11	12	13	14	15	16	17	18	19	20	21	22	23	24	25	26	27	28/29/30 31
DEC.	1	2	3	4	5	6	7	8	9	10	11	12	13	14	15	16	17	18	19	20	21	22	23	24	25	26	27	28/29/30 31

You can leave space in each square for the person who gets the calendar to enter their engagements or you can draw or paste little pictures in the spaces to mark special occasions, for instance:

A heart for St Valentine's day (14 February), a birthday cake for a family birthday, a rabbit for Easter, a Christmas tree, a shamrock for St Patrick's day (17 March), a leek for St David (1 March), a thistle for St Andrew (30 November), spring flowers for the spring holiday at the end of May, a sun for the late summer holiday at the end of August, or anything else which is appropriate for the person you are giving the calendar to.

This sort of calendar can be fixed to the wall with Sellotape or drawing pins, or Blu-tak.

Nine Men's Morris

This is a very ancient game, for which you can make your own board – or you can even draw one with chalk on concrete in summer or mark one out on the sand at the beach. You need two sets of counters of different colours – buttons, tiddlywinks or bottle tops will do.

Draw or paint the board on to a stiff square of cardboard, or a square of plywood. It should look like this:

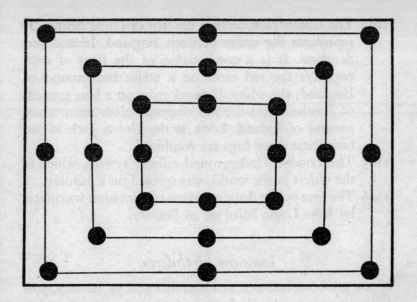

The game is for two players. They take it in turns to place one counter on the 'stations' on the board, trying to make lines of three or stop each other from making a line (rather like noughts and crosses). When all your nine counters are on the board, you can move your counters from one station to another along the lines to try to make other lines of three. From now on, whenever a player makes a line of three, he or she takes one of the other player's counters off the board.

The game ends when one player either has only two counters left on the board or has had all possible moves blocked by the other player's men.

It happened in January

1759 Robert Burns, the Scottish poet, was born on 25 January.
1788 The first issue of *The Times* newspaper was published on 1 January.

1801 The Union Jack became the flag of Great Britain. It represents the union between England, Ireland and Scotland. It is a combination of the flags of each country: the red cross on a white background of England; the white diagonal cross on a blue ground of Scotland and the red diagonal cross on a white ground of Ireland. Look at the Union Jack to see how these three flags are combined.

1863 The London Underground railway system, which is the oldest in the world, was opened on 1 January.

1926 The first public demonstration of television was given by John Logie Baird on 26 January.

January birthdays

If you are born between 22 December and 19 January, you fall within the astrological sign of Capricorn – the goat. According to this sign you will be ambitious and determined, but you will also be quiet, gentle and serious. You like routine and being well-organized. You are interested in practical hobbies and you are good at saving money.

Your birthstone is the garnet, which is usually a red or reddish-brown stone but, surprisingly, can also be green,

yellow or orange-red. Garnets are supposed to have powers of protecting people against illness and to endow their wearer with loyalty and light-heartedness.

In January your lucky colour is pink; your lucky number is three; and your lucky day is Thursday.

A riddle

White bird featherless
Flew from Paradise,
Perched on the castle wall;
Along came Lord Landless,
Took it up handless,
And rode away horseless
to the King's white hall.

Snow

JANUARY

My special days this month:

The weather this month:

The coldest day this month was:

The hottest day this month was:

In our park or garden I saw:

My Own Page

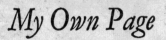

What I did this month indoors:

What I did this month outdoors:

The best/worst thing that happened this month:

Special events in the world this month:

FEBRUARY

February brings the rain,
Thaws the frozen ponds again.

The name of the month

The original Roman calendar had only ten months. It was extended to twelve by adding January and February by the Emperor Numa Pompilius. The name February came from a period of religious purification which was practised in Rome and was probably the predecessor of Christian Lent. Februare is the Latin word meaning 'to purify'.

Festivals

Candlemas or the Snowdrop Festival. The second of February is marked in the church calendar by Candlemas, a festival which represents the return of the light to the world after the dark winter months. You are halfway between the longest night in the year (21 December) and the spring equinox (21 March) when the hours of darkness and the hours of light are of equal length. This festival used to be marked by candles being blessed in the church and being held by the people during the Candlemas service.

6 *February* is the national day of New Zealand. Is it a winter or a summer holiday there?

St Valentine's Day. St Valentine was a priest who was killed because he sheltered Christians from the Romans who wanted to persecute them. The fourteenth of February is his saint's day and has become the day when friends and lovers exchange greetings and presents. Valentine cards were introduced in Victorian times. People used to say that this was the day on which birds began to choose their partners and build their nests.

> Muse, bid the morn awake,
> Sad winter now declines;
> Each bird doth choose a mate,
> This day St Valentine's.

Weather forecasts

There is an old Scots forecast about the weather which goes:

> If Candlemas Day be dry and fair,
> The half of winter's yet to come and mair;
> If Candlemas Day be wet and foul,
> The half of winter's gone since Yule.

Other sayings are, 'If the sun shines on Candlemas Day it will snow on May Day' (1 May), and 'All the months in the year curse a fair February.'

In this poem from Robert Chambers's *Book of Days* of 1863 is a list of the signs by which you can forecast foul weather.

The *hollow winds* begin to blow,
The *clouds look black*, the *glass is low*;
The *soot falls down*, the *spaniels sleep*;
And *spiders from their cobwebs peep*.
Last night *the sun went pale to bed*;
The *moon in haloes* hid her head.
The boding shepherd heaves a sigh,
For see a *rainbow* spans the sky.
The *walls are damp*, the *ditches smell*,
Closed is the pink-eyed *pimpernel*.
Hark! how the *chairs and tables crack*,
Old Betty's *joints are on the rack*;
Her *corns* with shooting pains *torment her*,
And to her bed untimely send her.
Loud quack the ducks, the *sea fowl cry*,
The *distant hills are looking nigh*.
How *restless* are the snorting *swine*!
The *busy flies disturb the kine*.
Low o'er the grass the swallow wings,
The *cricket*, too, *how sharp he sings*!
Puss on the hearth with velvet paws
Sits *wiping o'er her whiskered jaws*.
The *smoke* from chimneys right *ascends*,
Then spreading, back to earth it bends.
The *wind* unsteady *veers* around,
Or *settling in the south* is found.
The *sky is green*, the *air is still*,
The mellow *blackbird's voice is shrill*.
The *dog*, so altered in his taste,
Quits mutton bones, *on grass to feast*.
Behold the *rooks*, how odd their flight,
They imitate the *gliding* kite,
They seem *precipitate to fall*,
As if they felt the piercing ball.
The tender *colts on back do lie*,

Nor heed the travellers passing by.
In *fiery red the sun doth rise*,
Then *wades through clouds* to mount the skies.
'Twill surely rain, we see it with sorrow,
No working in the fields tomorrow.

The interesting thing about all these old 'saws' is that they
have a sound meteorological foundation. Some of them
are observations about what happens when the humidity
increases; some of them are caused by atmospheric pressure.
So remember this verse and watch the signs and see whether
you can outdo the weatherman!

Leap years

The earth goes round the sun in $365\frac{1}{4}$ days. We can't have a
quarter day in the calendar, so to get things straight we have
an extra day, 29 February, every fourth year. 1824 was a
leap year (as we call the year in which this extra day falls)
and February had five Sundays in it. This could not happen
again until the next time 1 February
fell on a Sunday. When was that or
when will it be?

If someone is travelling on 29
February it is supposed to be good
luck to give him or her a forget-me-
not.

Sunrise and sunset

By the end of February the sun is up just before 7.00 AM
and sets at about 5.30 PM. There are now over ten daylight
hours.

Nature notes

If there is a rookery near where you live, watch the rooks
beginning to rebuild their nests for another year. It is said

that if the rooks build high it will be a fair summer. You can begin now to see the winter wheat putting up green spikes in the ploughed fields. The hazel catkins are beginning to appear, before the leaves, on the hazel bushes. Early primroses and violets may be seen in the woods and along banks and hedgerows. Watch out for the 'February fair-maids' (snowdrops) in the garden.

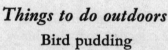

The snowdrop, in purest white array,
First rears its head on Candlemas day.

Things to do outdoors

Bird pudding

Make a wire-netting ball about the size of a grapefruit, using 1-inch wire netting. Then make up a mixture of stale brown bread crumbs, porridge oats or oatmeal, chopped nuts of all kinds, raisins, meat scraps and any wild-bird seed sold by your local pet shop. Now melt $\frac{1}{2}$ kilogram (1 pound) of any kind of dripping in an old saucepan; when it has melted and is hot, but not boiling, add your mixture of dry food and stir well. The consistency should be that of porridge or a thick stew. Then you put your wire-netting ball into the 'stew' and leave everything to set in a cool place. Your netting ball will come out a solid mass of attractive bird food which can hang by a chain or a wire wherever you can see the birds from your window.

An experiment with a bud

Plants are provided by nature with 'winter quarters' which protect them from the effects of cold. Some plants which die down to the root every autumn are now safely hidden underground. Shrubs and trees have all their tender growing parts closely sheltered in buds, which resist the frost. But their outer covering and the way in which the future leaves are closely wrapped inside is not the only way the bud is protected. You can prove this on a cold winter night. Take

a bud which has a strong covering (like one from a horse chestnut, sycamore or lime tree) and put it in a screw-top glass jar. Tie some string round the top of the jar and suspend it from the tree on which the bud grew on a really frosty night. The next morning the bud in the jar will have been penetrated and ruined by the cold, but the growing buds on the same tree will not have been injured at all. The 'mother tree' gives its buds more protection than is given by just the close wrapping of the 'winter quarters'. It is the life which is in the growing tree that gives this extra protection to the buds.

Things to do indoors

Make a Valentine Card

Valentine cards seem to fall into two categories – the sentimental and the comic. For a sentimental one you want lace, ribbons and red hearts (perhaps stuck on to the card with a piece of satin or velvet) and a little poem inside to your

friend. A comic one depends on your own sense of humour. My son received a beautiful card one year showing a working model of a heart taken from a biology book with the inscription 'My heart beats for you'. Sometimes the card itself is sentimental but the kick is in the message:

Roses are red,
Violets are blue,
Grass is green,
And so are you!

Make a present for your Valentine

What nicer present for a loved one than home-made sweets?
Even if you haven't got a Valentine, sweet-making is fun
and you can always eat them yourself!

Peppermint creams

You will need:
 ½ kilogram (1 lb) icing sugar
 1 egg
 juice from half a lemon
 a little peppermint essence

Sieve the icing sugar into a bowl to remove all the lumps.
Separate the yolk from the white of the egg by breaking the
egg into a saucer, placing an egg cup over the yolk and slip-
ping the white off into the bowl of icing sugar. Put the yolk
aside to use on another occasion. (If you leave it in the egg
cup and put some water in on top of it, it will keep better.)
Mix the egg white and the icing sugar together with a
wooden spoon. Then knead the mixture together with
your fingers until it is thoroughly combined; you need to
work hard at this. Add the lemon juice a drop at a time, so
that the mixture holds together well. Now add about half a
teaspoon of peppermint essence a drop at a time until you
get the taste you want. Press out the mixture on a cool surface until it is about 6 millimetres (¼ inch) thick. Cut it into
shapes using either a sweet-cutter or a knife, cutting squares,
triangles, diamonds and so on. Leave to harden – preferably overnight.

Chocolate fudge

You will need:

150 millilitres ($\frac{1}{4}$ pint) milk
28 grammes (1 ounce) butter or margarine
340 grammes ($\frac{3}{4}$ pound) sugar
3 tablespoons cocoa
Pinch salt
$\frac{1}{2}$ teaspoon vanilla

Mix everything together, except for the vanilla, in a saucepan. Heat until the sugar has dissolved, stirring gently all the time. Continue to heat until the mixture boils; let it boil gently until, when you drop a little of it from a spoon into a cup of cold water, you can gather it together into a soft ball. Remove the pan from the heat and allow the mixture to cool. While it is still quite warm, add the vanilla and beat the mixture hard until it is thick. Pour it into a greased tin, mark it out into squares, but leave it overnight before cutting.

Get well cards

February is a month for colds and 'flu, measles and sneezes, so you may want to make a little present to cheer a sick friend or one of the family. You either want to cheer them up with something amusing or give them something pleasant to look at while they are in bed. Here are two ideas, one of each kind.

A banner greeting

Take a piece of thread or string and some bits
of coloured paper, not too stiff, (but you will
probably need something a bit stiffer than
tissue paper). Cut out a number of little
triangular flags, like the ones that are used
in strings for carnivals.

They can be as small or as large as you wish, but will need
to have a flap at the wide end to wrap
them over the string, like this:

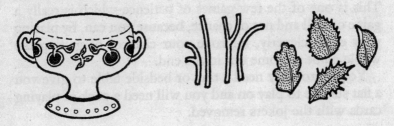

Write one letter of each word of your message on each and
then stick them on the string in order. You can send this
'card' through the post by folding each flag on top of the
one next to it.

A pot of flowers or a bowl of fruit

These are the traditional presents for taking to sick people
but you can give them in the form of a card. Using stiff
card, cut out a flower pot or bowl and then, with lighter-
coloured cards, cut out pieces to 'go into' the bowl. Stick
these in position. Here and overleaf are various stages in
the make-up of such a card:

Donna's Patience

If you are in bed yourself for a day or so, here's a game of patience which can keep you occupied for an hour or more. This is one of the few games of patience which is really a game of skill and not of chance, because you can, by placing your cards cleverly, improve your chances of getting the whole game to come out in the end.

You'll probably need a tray or bedside table to give you a flat surface to play on and you will need a pack of playing cards with the jokers removed.

Put out an ace, a two, a three and a four on the tray as shown on the left.

The aim of the game is to build up on these four cards in any suit so that the cards go up in ones on the ace (one), in twos on the two, in threes on the three and in fours on the four.

When you finish, if you get the game to come right out, your lines will be like this:

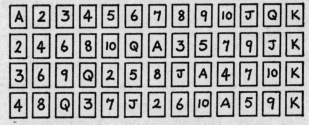

A	2	3	4	5	6	7	8	9	10	J	Q	K
2	4	6	8	10	Q	A	3	5	7	9	J	K
3	6	9	Q	2	5	8	J	A	4	7	10	K
4	8	Q	3	7	J	2	6	10	A	5	9	K

As you can see, each line is 13 cards long and ends with King.

To play, turn over the cards in the pack one at a time. If you turn over a card which fits one of the lines, put it there. For instance, if the first card you turn over is a six it can go after the three. If the card you turn up does not fit, you put it on one side. These discarded cards should be placed in four piles, face upward and in any order, like this:

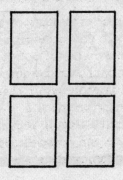

You can 'feed' on to the lines of cards either from the top of these piles or from the cards you turn over from the main pack, whenever there is a suitable card.

When you have played the game a few times, you'll begin to find that you can build up the four side piles in such a way that the cards will come off them in order, ready to go on to your lines. For instance, if you have put down a Queen on the side pile, try to get a Jack, 10 or 9 on top of it when that card comes up, so that when you have used these cards the Queen will be ready to use (Jack, then Queen on the Ace line, for instance).

It happened in February

1732 George Washington, the first American President, was born on 22 February.
1812 Charles Dickens was born on 7 February.
1927 The first solo trans-Atlantic flight was made by Captain Charles Lindbergh.
1969 The largest piece of stony meteorite which has ever been recovered fell in the USA. (*See* page 128 to read more about meteorites.)

February birthdays

If you are born between 20 January and 18 February, your sign of the zodiac is Aquarius – the water carrier. Aquarians are said to be always interested in what's going on around them, independent, stubborn and quick thinking. They are usually calm but they can lose their tempers. They are practical and logical in their thinking. They make friends easily.

Your birthstone is the clear violet-coloured amethyst. This stone, which represents sincerity and contentment, is also supposed to bring lasting happiness to lovers.

The lucky colour for Aquarians is orange; the lucky number is eight; the lucky day is Saturday.

The months of the year

Thirty days hath September,
April, June and November;
All the rest have thirty-one,
Excepting February alone,
And that has twenty-eight days clear
And twenty-nine in each Leap Year.

FEBRUARY

My special days this month:

The weather this month:

The coldest day this month was:

The hottest day this month was:

In our park or garden I saw:

My Own Page

What I did this month indoors:

What I did this month outdoors:

The best/worst thing that happened this month:

Special events in the world this month:

MARCH

March brings breezes loud and shrill,
Stirs the dancing daffodil.

The name of the month

March used to be the first month of the year – when spring is coming and life is really renewing itself. The Roman god

of war, Mars, was felt suitable to give his name to the first month because of the importance the Romans gave to war.

Festivals

St David's Day (1 March). St David is the patron saint of Wales whose symbol, the leek, is worn by Welshmen on this day.

St Patrick's Day (17 March). The patron saint of Ireland is commemorated by all good Irishmen, who wear the shamrock on this day.

Lent, which is the six-week period from Ash Wednesday to Easter Sunday, when Christians prepare for the commemoration of the death of Christ with fasting and other sacrifices, may start in February or March. The old Saxon name for March was Lenet-monat, meaning 'length month', when the days lengthened, and the word Lent may come from this.
Easter Sunday is always the first Sunday after the full moon which happens upon or next after 21 March. If the full moon is on a Sunday, Easter Day is the Sunday after. You can see from this, if you read it carefully, that the earliest Easter Day can be is the twenty-second of March. That is when the full moon falls on Saturday 21 March. Can you work out what is the latest day on which Easter can fall?

Mothering Sunday was the day on which, in olden times when many girls and young men went away from home to live in the houses and farms where they were employed, they were allowed to go home and visit their parents. This is the mid-Sunday in Lent, and it is followed by Care (or Passion) Sunday, Palm Sunday, and then Easter Sunday. The young people would take presents to their mothers on this visit and so the custom of giving your mother a present on this day has grown up.

Weather forecasts

Here are some traditional March sayings for you to check against the facts!

If March comes in like a lion, it goes out like a lamb.

March winds and April showers,
Make way for May flowers.

Dry March, wet April and cool May,
Fill barn and cellar and bring much hay.

March in January,
January in March, I fear.

Sunrise and sunset

21 March is the Spring Equinox, when the hours of daylight and the hours of darkness are equal. The sun will now be rising just before seven o'clock and setting at about seven o'clock in the evening. You now have four more hours of daylight than when you started making a record of these times early in January.

Summer Time

In the summer, we put our clocks and watches forward one hour, so that we have longer light evenings. We change our clocks on the morning of the third Sunday in March. Then we change them back one hour in the autumn on the fourth Sunday in October.

Nature notes

Even in the north of Britain, the new lambs will be appearing by now and in the south they are growing up well. The new grass is growing green in the meadows ready for the

cattle to be let out of the stock yards, where they have been fed during the winter. In a warm spring you may find the first frog spawn in a pond. Perhaps you may see some early swallows returning from their winter migration to Africa. Soon birds will be starting to make their nests. Watch out for them collecting grass and twigs. How early in the month are the spring flowers beginning to appear in gardens and parks?

Things to do outdoors

A mystery tour

Instead of deciding where you are going for a walk before you go, pick a route by chance and see where it takes you. Write directions on slips of paper, like: first left, second right, third left, and so on. Make two or three slips for each direction. Put the slips in a bowl and pick them out one at a time, with your eyes shut. Note down each direction in the order in which it comes out and then follow that route on your mystery tour.

Your eventual route, if you picked out five directions, might be: take the second left, first right, first left, second right, third right.

If you can't go in one of the directions because of a dead end, a major road or whatever, take the next direction on your list.

Another way to take this sort of walk is to put the slips of paper in your coat pocket, draw out one as you leave the house and follow it, then take the next one, and so on until you feel you have walked far enough.

Tadpoles

Towards the end of March the first frog spawn or frog's eggs may be found in ponds. Collect a few in a jar with some water from the pond. Put the spawn in a bigger bowl – a fish bowl or fish tank – when you reach home. Watch it

every day and record what you see – a hand magnifying lens will help your observations. First the tadpoles begin to develop inside the jelly which holds them and from which they feed; then they come out, and you should make sure that there are some water plants and tiny pinches of fish food in the bowl for them to feed on. Then the external gills appear like tiny tufts on each side of the head; then two legs sprout near the tail; then the forelegs appear, the tail is gradually absorbed into the body and the tiny frog is ready to come out of the water. Make sure there is a rock in the water at this stage so that the baby frog can climb out. Take your little frogs back to the pond when they are ready to come out of the water.

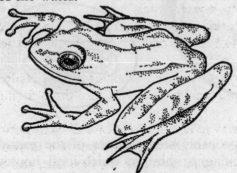

Things to do indoors

Pancake Day

The week immediately before Lent used to be celebrated with a final flurry of activity and feasting before the sober days of Lent began. This week was Carnival Week. (The word 'carnival' means 'farewell to meat', for 'carne' means meat and 'vale', farewell. During Lent no meat was eaten, of course.) One custom which still continues from these celebrations is the making of pancakes on Shrove Tuesday. Pancakes were cooked on this particular day because housewives could use up all the eggs and fat in the house in their making, in preparation for the Lenten fast.

You've probably seen pictures of the pancake race at Olney, Buckinghamshire, in which local housewives race through the town tossing their pancakes three times during the race. The winner is the first one to reach the church door with her pancake intact.

Perhaps you could run your own pancake race. But you'd better practise making them and tossing them first!

Pancakes

You will need:
  a thick frying pan, preferably with slightly sloping sides
  112 grammes (4 ounces) flour
  ½ teaspoon salt
  1 egg
  300 millilitres (½ pint) milk
  fat for frying

Sift the salt and flour together in a bowl. Make a well in the centre of the flour. Break the egg into this well and add half the milk.

Start from the centre of the mixture and working towards the outside, mix and beat thoroughly. Add the rest of the milk and stir it in. Leave the mixture to stand in a cool place for at least half an hour. Then pour it into a jug.

Heat a little fat in the frying pan, letting it melt and run all over the pan so that it is evenly coated with a very thin layer. Pour off any extra fat into a saucepan. Pour a little batter from the jug – just enough to cover the bottom of the pan thinly all over. Cook for a minute or two until it is brown underneath when you lift the edge with a palette knife or knife blade.

Now toss it!

To do this, pick up the frying pan, shake it a little to make sure that the pancake is lying loosely in the pan, then with a forward and backward movement of the arm, flip the pancake over. Of course, it's not as easy as this and, in my experience, many pancakes will end up on the edge of the pan – or on the floor. But persevere and you'll do it. If, however, you prefer safety, turn the pancake with a palette knife or fish slice.

Then cook it for a minute or two until it is brown on the other side. Serve with slices of lemon and a sprinkling of sugar.

Make your own barometer

A barometer measures air pressure. When the air pressure is high, the weather is fine; when the pressure is falling it is a sign that bad weather is coming. You can make quite a reliable barometer with a bit of an old balloon, a rubber band, a milk bottle and a straw. Stretch the piece of balloon tightly across the top of the bottle and fix it down with the rubber band. Glue the straw to the top of it so that the straw sticks out sideways. As the air pressure on the top of the bottle falls and rises, the other end of the straw will move.

Put the bottle in a position where the temperature will be much the same all the time. Fix a card to the wall, marking the high point and the low point and half a dozen points in between.

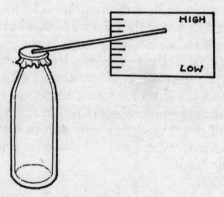

You will be able to forecast changes in the weather as the air pressure and the straw rise and fall.

A present for Mothering Sunday

A spring-flower picture

Take a piece of coloured card and some different-coloured papers – tissue paper or other thin paper will do fine. You will also need a pair of scissors and glue. First, on a scrap of paper plan a picture of a vase of flowers. You need not follow the plan exactly, but it will help you. Cut out green paper stems for the stems and leaves of your flowers. Fix these in position on the card, so that when you stick down the paper vase, they will come out of it in the right way. Then fix on all sorts of flowers, so that bits of them stand out from the card. There are some ideas on how to do this below. When all your flowers are in position, cut out a pot or bowl for the flowers and stick this over the stems to finish off the picture. Make two holes at the top of the card with a punch and thread a piece of ribbon through them, so that the picture can be hung up.

Here are some ideas on how to make the flowers.

Bell flowers: cut a half-circle of thin paper. Fold a quarter of it back on each side, so that you make a flat 'cone'. You can fringe the edges of the flower if you want to.

Using the flaps at the back, fix the flower on to your picture, so that it is raised from the card.

Fluffy flowers: cut out three layers of tissue paper and put them one on top of the other, like this:

Bunch them up and squeeze the bottom part together. Fix the flower on to your card and stick a tiny piece of green paper over the place where it joins the stem as a sepal, which will also cover the join.

Flowers with separate petals: cut out the petals and fix them separately on to the card. Fix on a centre in a contrasting colour, or you can use a button or a tiny

frill of tissue paper or lace at the centre. Below is the finished picture.

Easter cards

Many of the suggestions made for other cards in this book can be used with different designs to make Easter cards. You could make cut-out shapes of eggs, chicks and rabbits and use them to make cards like the ones described on page 178. You can make stand-up cards of spring flowers, Easter eggs and rabbits like those described on page 180.

You could also make a hanging card. Cut out various appropriate shapes like an Easter egg, a chicken, a pot of spring flowers, a rabbit. Colour them and decorate them in

any way that takes your fancy; a bit of ribbon and lace on the Easter egg, perhaps, the chicken made fluffy with yellow-dyed cotton wool, and so on. With a sharp needle make two holes at the head of each figure and then string them together with a needle and thread, spaced out and ready to be pinned up by the person who receives them.

A note of explanation on the back of the card ('stretch out the thread and fix each end to a shelf with Sellotape') might explain this rather unusual card.

Watching seeds grow

It is a little early to start planting things in the garden, but you can try some experiments with seeds in the house which will help you to understand what happens to the seeds you plant in the garden later.

A seed is like an egg. It has a covering, a store of food and a germ of life. To make this germ grow, you need water, warmth, air and darkness. You can see all this for yourself if you try this experiment with runner beans.

If you look closely at the beans you will see that there is a little hole in the covering through which they can take in

water. Put your beans in a saucer of water for about three days. They will begin to swell with the water they have taken in through that little hole. Now plant them in a box of earth. The seed will now have darkness and, so long as you don't crush the soil down too firmly, it will have air. After about a week dig up one bean. Has it put down a root yet? Dig up one of your beans every few days to watch how the root develops and how a shoot grows up and eventually pushes through the surface of the earth.

If you put a ruler in the box next to the plants, you will be able to measure how quickly the plant grows day by day. You could make a record of the findings of your experiment, showing the dates and your observations.

Another way to watch a plant growing is to put a piece of blotting paper round the inside of a glass jar. Put some soaked beans between the blotting paper and the glass. Keep a little water in the jar so that the blotting paper absorbs it and takes it to the seeds. Watch the beans and see how first the root and then the sprout appear.

You can prove that plants 'drink' water if you take a pot of water and dye it with red ink. Then stand a twig with leaves in the red water. Look at it the next day and see how the twig has drunk up the red water and the veins in its leaves have gone reddish in colour.

Buds

Bring some budding twigs into the house. Break them off the tree as carefully as you can. Put them in a vase of water and watch the new leaves slowly unfurl as they are doing on the trees.

See if you can find a sheltered street or corner of a field where the spring comes early. We used to walk down a street on the way home from school each day where spring came fully a month earlier than it did in other, less sheltered, streets.

It happened in March

44 BC Julius Caesar was assassinated in Rome on 15 March (the Ides of March).

1474 Michelangelo, the great Italian painter, sculptor and architect, is said to have been born on 6 March 1474.

1675 A start was made on the construction of the Greenwich Observatory. The building was completed a year later and King Charles II made Freedman the first Astronomer Royal. The line of the Greenwich Meridian, from which times around the world are taken, passes through Greenwich, and if you go there you can stand with one foot on either side of the Meridian.

March birthdays

If you are born between 19 February and 20 March, your zodiac sign is Pisces – the fish. People born under this sign are said to be creative and restless, with little thought for the future. They are charming and good-natured, but they don't like routine or discipline. The birthstone for March is either the aquamarine or the bloodstone. Aquamarine takes its name from the Latin words for water and the sea and, with

its clear blue-green colour, it is like the sea on a fine summer day. The aquamarine is the sailor's stone, promising protection from the perils and monsters of the oceans. The bloodstone is a dark green stone flecked with red. Bloodstone used to be thought to have the power of making its wearer invisible, but it was also said to give courage and wisdom.

Your lucky number is three; your lucky colour is pink; your lucky day is Thursday.

Birds' nests

The skylark's nest among the grass
And waving corn is found;
The robin's on a shady bank,
With oak leaves strewn around.

The martins build their nests of clay
In rows beneath the eaves;
While silver lichens, moss and hair,
The chaffinch interweaves.

The cuckoo makes no nest at all,
But through the wood she strays
Until she finds one snug and warm,
And there her egg she lays.

Rooks build together in a wood,
And often disagree;
The owl will build inside a barn
Or in a hollow tree.

The blackbird's nest of grass and mud
In brush and bank is found;
The lapwing's darkly spotted eggs
Are laid upon the ground.

Birds build their nests from year to year,
According to their kind,
Some very neat and beautiful,
Some easily designed.

                         Anon

MARCH

My special days this month:

The weather this month:

The coldest day this month was:

The hottest day this month was:

In our park or garden I saw:

My Own Page

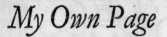

What I did this month indoors:

What I did this month outdoors:

The best/worst thing that happened this month:

Special events in the world this month:

April brings the primrose sweet,
Scatters daisies at our feet.

The name of the month

It is possible that April's name comes from the Latin word 'aperio', meaning 'I open', referring to the opening of the

buds and flowers. Another suggestion is that it is named after the Greek goddess of love, Aphrodite, the name being changed by the Romans to Aphrilis.

Festivals

April Fool's Day (*1 April*). 'It is customary on this day for boys to practise jocular deceptions. When they succeed, they laugh at the person whom they think they have rendered ridiculous and exclaim, "Ah, you April Fool!" ' So William Hone reported in his *Everyday Book* in 1826. Of course, girls too make April fools on this day.

The sort of tricks played on this day are sending someone to buy an imaginary article, like a pennyworth of 'incle'; saying 'Your shoe-lace is undone,' or 'You've a dirty mark on your face.' The idea is to catch someone off his guard or to pass off on him a simple fact which is not true.

Easter. Look back at March to see how the date of Easter is fixed.

At Easter time we remember the death of Christ upon the cross on Good Friday and on Easter Sunday we celebrate His rising from the dead.

But Easter is also the spring festival when new life comes to the earth. The symbols of Easter represent this rebirth – eggs, flowers and young animals.

Eggs were believed to bring life to the new crops planted in the spring and in many countries were buried in the fields at planting time. Finnish peasants used to carry an egg in their pocket while they ploughed the land in the spring. In Russia, Easter Day was set aside for visiting. People went from house to house, giving an egg to their hosts and receiving one in return. After the isolation of the long Russian winter, this was the time when farm life and social life began again and this life of the new year was symbolized by the eggs.

An old North Country Easter custom is that of egg-rolling competitions. No one seems to know the origins of this custom, but basically you compete in rolling hard-boiled eggs down a sloping field or hill. (If you cook your egg for half an hour in preparation it will keep almost indefinitely.)

St George's Day is 23 April. St George is the patron saint of England.

Weather forecasts

'A cold April the barn will fill.' If April is cold, is there really a good harvest in August and September?

'Easter in snow;
Christmas in mud;
Christmas in snow;
Easter in mud.'

Record whether or not Easter is in a wet period and see what the Christmas weather will be like. As Easter can be at any time from the end of March to late April, this forecast is less definite than many.

'If the ash comes out before the oak,
Then the summer will be a soak;
If the oak comes out before the ash,
Then the summer will be a splash.'

Watch to see which comes out first. And also watch for the flowering of the ash, the oak, the poplar, the larch and other trees. Did you know that these trees flowered?

Sunrise and sunset

By the end of April the sun is up by a quarter to six and has not set until after eight o'clock.

Nature notes

The trees and hedges are really becoming green now and grow more so as the month progresses. The horse chestnut is among the first of the trees to be in full leaf. Watch as the oak leaves, which start as a reddish colour, change to green.

The nightingale is only in Britain briefly, but if you are lucky you may hear his song on a moonlit night from April onwards.

Things to do outdoors

Keep a wind record

'When the wind is in the east,
'Tis neither good for man nor beast;
When the wind is in the north,
The skilful fisher goes not forth;
When the wind is in the south,
It blows the bait in the fish's mouth;
When the wind is in the west,
Then 'tis at the very best.'

If you have a wind vane on the roof of a nearby building, notice which way the wind is blowing and see how true you think this verse is.

If you wet your finger and hold it up, you can tell from which direction the wind is blowing, for that side of your finger will dry the quickest.

Of course winds can be strong or they can be so weak that you are hardly aware of them. An admiral who lived in the eighteenth century made a scale of winds, called the Beaufort Scale after him. Make a record each day of the winds according to your assessment of the Beaufort Scale.

	Force effects	*Description*	*Miles per hour*
0	Smoke rises straight up from the chimneys	Calm	less than 1
1	Smoke drifts	Light	1–3
2	Wind is felt on the face, leaves of the trees rustle	Light	4–7
3	Light flags are extended	Light	8–12
4	Raises dust, moves small branches	Moderate	13–18
5	Small leafy trees sway	Fresh	19–24
6	Large branches move	Strong	25–31
7	Trees sway	Gale	32–38
8	Twigs break off trees, difficult to walk	Gale	39–46
9	Chimney pots are blown down	Gale	47–54
10	Trees are uprooted, branches broken	Strong gale	55–63
11	Widespread damage of a kind rare in Britain	Strong gale	64–75
12	Devastation	Hurricane	75 +

Things to do indoors

Decorating Easter eggs

There are all sorts of different ways to decorate eggs. Here are a few of them.

Wax patterns

Draw patterns on the egg shells with a wax crayon or the pointed end of a candle. Then put the eggs in a cold water dye overnight. When you boil them for breakfast the wax will melt, leaving white patterns on the dyed shells.

A blown egg

Blow the yolk and white from the egg so only the shell remains. You can do this by making a small hole at one end and a larger hole at the other. Then blow through the small hole so that the contents are blown out of the larger hole – on to a saucer which you've placed to catch them. Then place the egg upright on a piece of Plasticine so that you can decorate it with paint or a felt-tip pen directly on to the shell.

Dyed egg

Or you could dye it. Vegetable colouring for Easter egg dyeing can be bought from a grocer's shop in a variety of colours – deep pink cochineal, green, yellow and purple, among others. But you can also make your own dyes. Tie your egg in an onion skin wrapped in a piece of muslin, then boil it. It will come out a yellowy-brown with the pattern of the onion skin printed on it. Experiment with dyes from such things as beetroot, coffee grounds, oak leaves, bracken. First boil your dyeing agent so that the water is coloured as darkly as possible. You will need to experiment with this. Then boil the eggs in the coloured water. Experiment with other leaves and dyeing agents to see what happens. Draw patterns or faces on the eggs with a pencil before you boil them, or with a felt-tip pen afterwards. Rub the eggs over with a drop of cooking oil to make them shine.

Egg people

Hard-boil the eggs with some cochineal, coffee grounds or other colouring in the water, to make them the colour of skin. Then, when they are cool, draw or paint faces on them. Put a little glue on the top and the sides so that you can stick cotton wool or wool hair on the eggs. Fix your egg faces on to a circle of paper for a neck and colour it. You can decorate the Easter table with them and then eat them in a salad the next day!

Here are some egg people to give you ideas for your own.

Sugar Easter eggs

You can use this mixture to make Easter eggs or to make sugar mice for presents at other times.

You will need:
  225 grammes (½ lb) icing sugar
  the white of an egg

Separate the yolk of the egg from the white as described on page 33. Put the yolk aside to use on another occasion and add the egg white a little at a time to the icing sugar in a mixing bowl. Remember that any liquid goes a long way in icing sugar and that it is very easy to make it too runny. If it does get runny, add more icing sugar. Mix the sugar and egg together into a stiff paste. Take it out of the bowl, knead it thoroughly on a board and then mould it into little Easter eggs. You can colour your eggs by separating the paste into different little bowls and adding a few drops of colouring which you mix and knead in. If you want to make sugar mice, you will need some cochineal colouring. Mould the mice from the sugar mixture, then fix a little piece of string on to the bodies for a tail and colour the eyes and inside of the ears with cochineal so that they are pink.

Easter eggs

There were certainly not as many Easter eggs about when I was small. I can remember very vividly the time that we had our first Easter eggs. Three big, square, pink and silver boxes appeared at the breakfast table on Easter Sunday. Inside each box was a beautiful football-sized chocolate egg. I ate mine almost immediately in a frenzy of gluttony. My very organized little sister incubated hers in the box and it lasted for months. Regularly she would take it out of the box, inspect it, and then tidily pack it up again. In midsummer it started to wilt. After a great deal of bullying I was allowed to smash it and I helped her eat it. My baby brother was absolutely amazed by his egg. He took it out of the box and crawled round it. Unfortunately he stood up to smile and, not being too steady, he toppled over and sat directly on top of it. In the shock and horror of the moment his eyes and mouth opened and shut in complete disbelief, then when he realized what he had done the tears started to run down his face and he cried for hours.

Nicky Browne
(*Teacher's World*)

Easter biscuits

These traditional Easter biscuits used to be tied together in groups of three with ribbon, so that each bundle of biscuits represented the Trinity of the Father (God), Son (Jesus) and Holy Spirit.

You will need:
    225 grammes (8 ounces) self-raising flour
    113 grammes (4 ounces) margarine or butter
    116 grammes (4 ounces) sugar
    56 grammes (2 ounces) currants
    Pinch of salt
    A little grated lemon peel
    1 egg

This will be enough to make thirty biscuits about 5 centimetres (2 inches) across.

Sift together the flour and salt and then rub the margarine into the flour with your fingers. Add the sugar, lemon rind and currants and then mix them all together with the egg (which you have already beaten). Knead the mixture into a

firm paste. It will get rather stiffer if you then put it aside for about an hour before you roll it out. Roll the mixture out on a lightly floured board so that it is about 6 millimetres ($\frac{1}{4}$ inch) thick. Use a biscuit-cutter or small cup to cut the dough into biscuits. Put the circles on to a greased biscuit tray and bake in the oven at electricity 375° or gas Mark 4, for about fifteen minutes. Put the biscuits on to a wire tray to cool when they are a light golden brown colour.

Easter presents

An egg

When your mother is next using eggs for cooking, ask her to save two halves of an egg shell for you. Ask her to crack them apart very carefully so that the edges won't be too ragged. Wash out the two halves and let them dry. Fix the egg back together at the crack and bind Sellotape carefully round the join. Decorate the newly made egg with paint, stick on pictures and tie a ribbon round the middle to cover the join.

You could make four or five eggs like this and place them in a mossy nest as an Easter table decoration.

A basket of sugar eggs

Make a little basket out of stiff coloured paper, as follows. Cut out this shape:

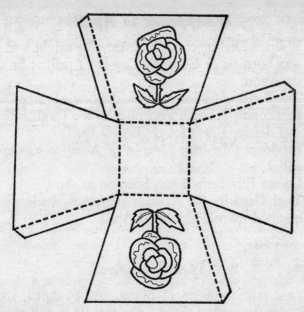

Score the paper along the dotted lines. Draw or stick pictures on to the outside of the basket at this stage. Be sure the pictures are on the side that will be the outside. Fold up the basket and stick the flaps on the inside, so that the basket stands up.

Put on a handle, like this:

Fill the basket with sugar Easter eggs (see page 67 for the recipe).

You could make little baskets like this for sweets on a party table or even smaller ones to hang on a Christmas tree filled, with Smarties.

A bowl of spring flowers

On page 149 there are instructions for making a bowl of bulbs for Christmas. You could follow these instructions but plant your bulbs in January or February, so that you would have them ready for Easter time.

It happened in April

1564 William Shakespeare, the great playwright and poet, was born on St George's Day (23 April) at Stratford on Avon.

1746 The Battle of Culloden at which Bonnie Prince Charlie, the Young Scottish Pretender to the English throne, was defeated, was fought on 16 April.

1865 President Abraham Lincoln of America was assassinated.

1926 Queen Elizabeth II was born on 21 April.

1961 Yuri Gagarin, the Russian astronaut, made the first manned space flight on 12 April.

April birthdays

If you are born between 21 March and 19 April, you are born under the sign of Aries – the ram. It is said that you will be straightforward but also determined, friendly and talkative, imaginative and honest. You enjoy a challenge, but will not always follow a good example. You can be rather bossy, and although you easily feel hurt, you are not always as sensitive as you might be about others' feelings.

Your birthstone is the diamond – one of the most precious and expensive of all gem stones. Diamonds are supposed to bring good luck and happiness and to give strength of character to their wearer.

Your lucky colour is brown; your lucky number four; and your lucky day is Wednesday.

Spring song

For, lo, the winter is past,
The rain is over and gone;
The flowers appear on the earth;
The time of the singing of birds is come,
And the voice of the turtle dove
   Is heard in our land;
The fig tree puts forth her green figs,
And the vines with the tender grape
   Give a good smell.

From the Song of Solomon

A riddle

In marble walls as white as milk,
Lined with a skin as soft as silk,
Within a fountain crystal clear,
A golden apple doth appear.
No doors there are to this stronghold,
Yet thieves break in and steal the gold.

An egg

APRIL

My special days this month:

The weather this month:

The coldest day this month was:

The hottest day this month was:

In our park or garden I saw:

My Own Page

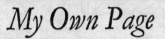

What I did this month indoors:

What I did this month outdoors:

The best/worst thing that happened this month:

Special events in the world this month:

May brings flocks of pretty lambs,
Skipping by their fleecy dams.

The name of the month

This month was named after Majores, the senior (or major) branch of the government assembly or senate in Rome.

Festivals

May Day. We seldom now see May Day (1 May) celebrated as it once was. This was the day on which the end of winter and the full opening of the new flowers were celebrated. People used to dance round a flower-decked maypole, which was the symbol of the new life pushing up from under the earth.

It was said that the dew on the fields on May Morning was a cure for skin ailments:

> The fair maid who, on first of May,
> Goes to the fields at break of day,
> Washes in dew from hawthorn tree,
> Will ever after handsome be.

May Day has now come to be celebrated as a day of solidarity among workers, with processions and parades.

Weather forecasts

A dry May and a leaking June
Make the farmer whistle a merry tune.

Why do you think that this is so? But here is a different description of what is needed to make the farmer happy:

Mist in May, and heat in June,
Make the harvest right soon.

When the dew is on the grass,
Rain will never come to pass.

Rain before seven,
Fine before eleven.

Sunrise and sunset

The sun will now be rising by about a quarter past five and it will not set until nine o'clock in the evening, so you now have sixteen hours of daylight.

Nature notes

The sheep are shorn in May and you can see them flat-coated in the fields. The pink and white 'candles' of the horse chestnut trees appear among the fresh green leaves. Try to go to a bluebell wood in early May, but bring back only the lasting memory of what you have seen, not the fast-wilting flowers. Yellow cowslips appear later in the month. Nestlings are beginning to appear. Watch how busy the parent birds are now, collecting food for them.
Listen for the cuckoo:

The cuckoo comes in April,
He sings his song in May;
In the middle of June
He changes his tune,
And then he flies away.

The cuckoo is a largish bird, with pointed wings and a long tail. It is blue-grey in colour with barred black and white underparts. It is only the male bird which makes the well-known 'cuckoo'. The female bird lays ten to twelve eggs a year, but she lays them in other birds' nests! When the nestlings hatch, they soon grow bigger than the other nestlings in the nest. They demand more food than the other babies because of their size and keep their poor 'foster' parents desperately busy. Often they push their 'foster' brothers and sisters out of the nest, too.

Things to do outdoors

Making a sun clock

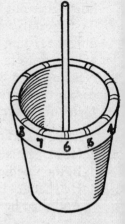

Fix a long stick into the central hole of a flower pot. Put the pot in a position where it will be in the sun all day. As the sun moves round, the shadow of the stick will move along the edge of the pot. Have a pot of white paint and a small brush ready and, at each hour during the day, go and mark a line on the pot where the shadow of the stick falls. When you have done this for every daylight hour, you will be able to use your sun clock on sunny days to tell the time.

Field mushrooms

There are all sorts of edible mushrooms growing wild and these are a great treat in the summer, but you must have advice from a book or a naturalist on how to identify the edible ones from the poisonous ones. **Never** eat an unidentified mushroom. The ones to avoid are the Death Cap with its light yellow cap, the Fly Agaric with its scarlet cap with white scales (the very picture of a fairy toadstool) and the Purple Agaric with its purple, slightly crinkled cap. The Verdigris Agaric with its bright green and very beautiful cap and the Yellow-staining Mushroom with its yellow spots are also poisonous. The last one is particularly dangerous because it is not unlike the common edible field mushroom.

Things to do indoors

Give a party

A lot of people have birthdays in the summer, so here are some ideas for parties – although many of the ideas would be suitable for other times of the year too.

What do you need to make a party? Friends, food and something to do. So let's look at a few ideas, first for inviting your friends; then for feeding them and decorating the table to make the food even more mouth-watering; and lastly, a few ideas for things to do at a party.

Table decorations

You can use paper chains to link each person to the centre-piece, which might be a candlestick made from a bottle wreathed with leaves and flowers. You can put little bowls of flowers before each person or have a central flower decoration, but this must be low enough to see over or it interrupts conversation! Put another flower in each napkin.

A basket or bowl of fruit can look lovely on the table – and can be eaten by the guests at the end of the meal.

Crackers

You can make your own crackers. You will need crêpe paper, corrugated paper, ribbon and tiny presents to put inside. Take a piece of corrugated paper about 9 centimetres wide and 12·5 centimetres long (3 inches wide by 5 inches long). Wrap it in a cylinder around the present (which could be wrapped in tissue paper to make the unwrapping more exciting). Take a piece of crêpe paper about 15 by 25 centimetres (6 by 10 inches). Wrap this round the cylinder of corrugated paper and glue the side where it joins. Tie the cracker with ribbon at each end.

Wrap a contrasting strip of paper round the middle, fix it and stick a little picture on it.

Use paper to match the summer flowers you use on the table.

Paper cups

You can make paper cups serve as place cards. The simplest way to do this is to use ordinary white paper cups and just paint people's names on to them in bright colours.

Napkin rings

Paper napkins can be folded and stood up on the plates or in the glasses, or you can make napkin rings for them. Take a strip of coloured cartridge paper 8 by 10 centimetres (3 by 4 inches). Roll it into a tube and glue or staple it together. Take a bit of tissue paper 10 by 15 centimetres (4 by 6 inches). Fold it in half so that it measures 10 by 8 centimetres (4 by 3 inches). Fringe the open side, like this:

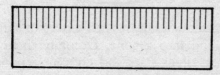

Glue the closed side round the edge of the card ring and open out the fringe. Paste a picture on the roll or the initial of one of your guests. Put the napkins in their rings.

Paper hats

You can make your own paper hats quite simply, though it is also possible to make quite ambitious ones. Here are two simple ones.

Crowns: cut a strip of paper about 11 centimetres (4½ inches) wide and long enough to go round your head. Cut one edge of it to make the points of a crown. Stick on 'jewels' made of coloured paper, outlined in glue on to which

'glitter' can be sprinkled. Every crown can be a slightly different shape and have different 'jewels' if everyone is going to be 'royalty'.

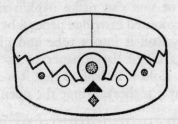

Clowns' or witches' hats: cut big half-circles of stiff paper and fold them round into a cone. Decorate them with large coloured spots, silver stars and crescent moons and fix a tassel of crêpe paper to the top.

Food for a summer party

What to eat? 'Lots' is often the best answer. There's nothing like enough to make people satisfied; and nothing like too little to make people feel dissatisfied. It's probably a good idea therefore to have a few easy-to-make 'fillers' and two or three special things. In this way you satisfy people's appetites without exhausting yourself with the preparations.

EASY-TO-MAKE 'FILLERS'

Baked potatoes; potato crisps; peanuts; grilled sausages (served hot or cold, alone or in buns); cheese biscuits.
Sandwiches. Here are some ideas for fillings:

> Hard-boiled eggs mashed up with mayonnaise; lettuce and tomato; sardines mashed up with lemon juice; ham; cheese and tomato; fish or meat paste and tomato; peanut butter and lettuce; tinned salmon and cucumber; cheese and chutney; cream cheese and chives; mashed banana; peanut butter and tomato sauce; cucumber.

Make little flags showing by words or pictures what the sandwiches have inside them. Stick them on toothpicks and place them on the plates of sandwiches.

Open sandwiches. Open sandwiches, which originate in Scandinavia where they are called Smørgasbord, are more difficult to make because they have to be decorated individually, but this can be made easier if you have a *tube* of mayonnaise, a tube of cream cheese and a tube of pink-coloured spread to help you in the work.

Cut slices of bread from a day-old loaf, butter them lightly and then cover with a thin layer of cream cheese or mayonnaise. Or you can use cream crackers or other biscuits. Decorate with:

Ham, sliced cucumber and mayonnaise decorations; scrambled egg, parsley and mayonnaise decorations; mashed-up salmon at one end, layers of sliced cucumber and mayonnaise at the other; sardines laid diagonally across the bread with slices of tomato at the corners; sliced tomato decorated with cream cheese; tinned sliced meat decorated with sliced olives or pickled cucumber and mayonnaise.

A horizontal sandwich loaf. Take a day-old loaf of brown or white bread. Cut it in slices *horizontally* (i.e. the opposite way from usual). Butter the slices, then spread fillings between the layers. Use only two or three varieties of filling for each loaf, for instance: top layer sliced meat; next layer scrambled egg and mayonnaise; next layer lettuce and mayonnaise; then repeat these layers. Store the loaf until

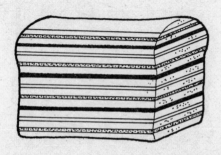

shortly before the party with a slight weight on top to hold the layers together. Then cut the loaf *vertically* so that each slice is striped across. Serve straight on to plates, so the sandwiches won't crumble.

If your party tea is late-ish, you could add:

A big bowl of salad with lots of lettuce, quartered tomatoes, radishes and spring onions, sprinkled with parsley, served with a bowl of salad dressing.

A bowl of potato salad or a bowl of rice salad (cooked rice mixed with sultanas, chopped-up tinned red pimento and cooked peas or corn; mix it while the rice is hot and then allow it to cool).

AND THEN SOME 'SPECIALS':

Picnic jellies. Keep your yoghurt or cream cups to use as containers; they make it much easier to eat jellies out of doors. Make a jelly with fruit added while it is hot (orange with a tin of mandarins; raspberry with a tin of raspberries; lemon with sliced peaches). Let it cool a bit before pouring it into the yoghurt cups to set.

Stuffed eggs. Hard-boil one or two eggs for each guest. Cool them in cold water and shell them. Cut in half lengthwise and scoop out the yolks. Mash these in a bowl, add salt and pepper and ½ teaspoonful mayonnaise for each egg.

Add ¼ teaspoon curry powder for three eggs. Then put the yolk mixture back into the half egg whites. Sprinkle them with paprika pepper and scatter chopped parsley over the top.

Fruit cup. This recipe is enough for ten glasses; increase the quantities if you need more.

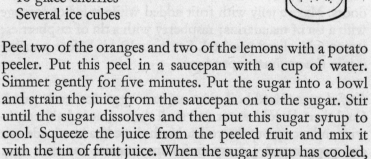

You will need:
   3 lemons
   3 oranges
   56 grammes (2 ounces) sugar
   1 can pineapple or apple juice
   1 cup water
   1 pint soda water or ginger ale
   10 glacé cherries
   Several ice cubes

Peel two of the oranges and two of the lemons with a potato peeler. Put this peel in a saucepan with a cup of water. Simmer gently for five minutes. Put the sugar into a bowl and strain the juice from the saucepan on to the sugar. Stir until the sugar dissolves and then put this sugar syrup to cool. Squeeze the juice from the peeled fruit and mix it with the tin of fruit juice. When the sugar syrup has cooled, mix it with the fruit juice. Slice the third orange and the third lemon very thinly for decoration.

Just before serving, add the ice cubes, soda water (or ginger ale), the glacé cherries and the slices of orange and lemon. Serve from a big bowl with a ladle; if you try to pour from a jug the fruit and ice will splash out into the glasses or stay determinedly in the jug.

And something to do: party games

Prepare a list of the games you want to play and make sure you have collected any equipment you may need.

GAMES TO BREAK THE ICE

Who's who? Ask each guest to bring a picture of himself as a baby. Pin the photographs up, in cellophane envelopes so they won't get marked, and let the guests guess who is who.

Who am I? Make a label for each person with the name of a famous character on it. When the guests arrive, pin a name on each person's back. They then have to go round asking questions of the other guests in order to find out who they are.

Traditional games. Just a reminder of some of the games you might play: pin the tail on the donkey; musical chairs; pass the parcel; blindman's buff; hide and seek; treasure hunt; charades.

(For a whole selection of party games, look at the *Piccolo Book of Parties and Party Games* by Deborah Manley and Peta Rée.)

It happened in May

1519 Leonardo da Vinci, the great Italian painter, sculptor, architect and engineer, was born on 2 May.

1819 Queen Victoria was born on 24 May.

1840 The first issue of adhesive stamps was made on 6 May.

1926 The General Strike in Britain lasted from 4–12 May.

1953 Mount Everest was climbed by Edmund Hillary and the Nepalese sherpa Tenzing on 29 May. The news reached Britain on the morning of the Queen's Coronation on 2 June.

May birthdays

If you are born between 20 April and 20 May, your sign is Taurus – the bull. And your character is said to be rather like that of a bull – strong and silent, but if pressed you can become obstinate and, if roused, can be as 'mad as a bull'. Taurians like to mind their own business, and they are methodical and industrious.

Your birthstone, the emerald, reflects the green of the month.

Of all green things which bounteous earth supplies,
Nothing in greenness with the emerald vies.

The emerald is a symbol of peace of mind and calm happiness. Your lucky day is Sunday; your lucky number is eight; and your lucky colour is green.

May song

Up, up, let us greet
The season so sweet,
   For winter is gone,
And the flowers are springing,
And little birds singing,
Their soft notes ringing,
   And bright is the sun!
Where all was dressed
In a snowy vest,
There grass is growing
With dew-drops glowing,
   And flowers are seen
   On beds so green.
              Godfrey of Nifen
              (thirteenth century)

MAY

My special days this month:

The weather this month:

The coldest day this month was:

The hottest day this month was:

In our park or garden I saw:

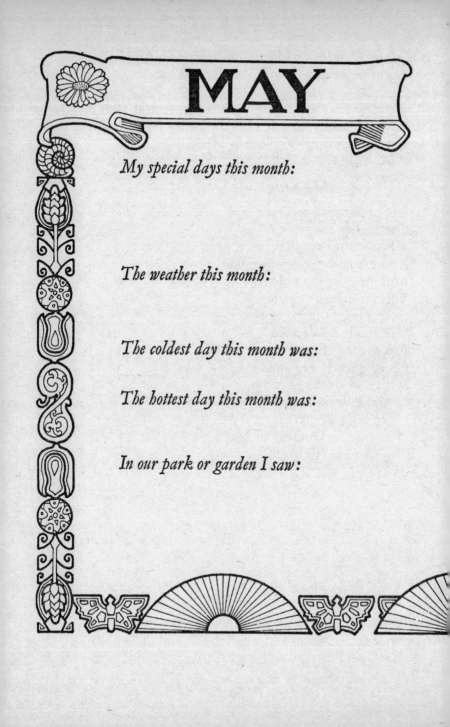

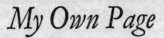

My Own Page

What I did this month indoors:

What I did this month outdoors:

The best/worst thing that happened this month:

Special events in the world this month:

June brings tulips, lilies, roses,
Fills the children's hands with posies.

The name of the month

June was named after the junior branch of the Roman government assembly, Juniores.

Festivals

The Queen's Official Birthday is celebrated on 2 June, although her real birthday is in April.

Midsummer Day (24 June). You might like to renew an old custom with a Midsummer bonfire party.

Weather forecasts

If you are going to be out and about, and especially if you are going on a picnic or to the seaside for a day, you want to know about the weather. Here are some guidelines for the next day's weather.

In the waning of the moon,
A cloudy moon – fair afternoon.

Evening red and morning grey,
Send the traveller on his way.
Evening grey and morning red,
Bring the rains upon his head.

A summer fog is for fair weather.

Watch the clouds for signs of what is to come:

If woolly fleeces spread the heavenly way,
No rain, be sure, disturbs the summer day.

A round-topped cloud with flattened base carries rainfall in that base.

Sunrise and sunset

On 21 June (the longest day of the year) the sun rises before 5 o'clock and does not set until about twenty past nine. Watch carefully now as the days begin to grow shorter.

Nature notes

This is the month for haymaking so the farmers are waiting anxiously for a spell of dry weather.

See if you can find a yellow toad-flax, like a small garden snapdragon, in the grass. There will be buttercups and daisies in the fields now too. Have you ever made a daisy chain?

You may be lucky enough to see mallard ducklings and young moorhens like fluffy little black tugboats if you are near a pond or stream. Watch out for the hovering dragon-fly too.

Magpies

In the summer, magpies are in the fields, flashing over the hedges and roads with their black and white plumage. An old verse says of sighting magpies:

One is sorrow,
Two is mirth,
Three is a wedding,
Four is a birth,
Five is silver,
Six is gold,
Seven is a secret
Never to be told.

So when you are travelling round on a summer day the number of magpies you see tells your fortune.

Things to do outdoors

Time for a picnic

Our family goes on picnics when the weather looks right, not just in the summer. So we've had picnics in March – sitting on the grass under leafless trees – and we've had picnics in November with a bonfire. And there's no reason not to have a picnic on a sunny day in the snow so long as you are properly prepared for it. But, of course, summer is the time for picnics. So here are some ideas for picnic making in June, though you can use the ideas for any sunny day.

Regular picnickers should keep everything they need together in one place as far as possible, with a check list which can be gone through quickly to make sure they don't find themselves in a Yorkshire dale with a tin but no opener or on the South Downs with a hard-boiled egg but no salt.

Here is a useful basic check list, but you may want to add or subtract things to suit your own family's ways.

Equipment	*Food*
Tin opener	Salt and pepper
Knives	Sugar
Spoons and forks	Milk
Plastic bottles for drinks	Butter
Plates or bowls	Salad dressing
A tea towel	
Butter box	
Napkins (paper)	

There are lots of different sorts of picnics and they need different sorts of preparation.

For a picnic on a long day's walking it is more important to be carefully prepared yourself and not to be carrying too much than to have a good meal. Nuts, chocolates, condensed milk and raisins are delicious and sustaining on a hill-walking expedition, and you won't use up much energy in carrying them.

And this seems to me – on most occasions – an important rule for picnics: don't overload yourselves. How often have you seen people picnicking in a layby by a stream of fume-belching traffic or near a car park at the beach because they had too much gear to make it worth their while to move 100 yards to a nice place? Picnicking doesn't have to be primitive and uncomfortable, but nor does it have to be an occasion when one needs a mule train to carry the clobber!

Picnics are about two things basically – about being outside and about eating.

Let's look first at the eating.

Basic food

hard-boiled eggs; hot or cold grilled or fried sausages; slices of cold meat; crisps; cheese; sausage rolls; bread and butter; lettuce and tomatoes; cucumber, spring onions, radishes, watercress; apples, oranges, bananas; cake and biscuits; fruit squash, tea, milk, coffee.

Other food

Sandwiches – see page 83 for fillings.

Rice salad. Cook 56 grammes (2 ounces) rice for each person in boiling, salted water. Let it cool, but don't let it get quite cold. Cook 112 grammes (4 ounces) frozen peas. Open a tin of sweetcorn and put the contents to drain in a sieve. Slice up half a tomato per person in little bits. With a sharp knife or kitchen scissors, cut up one spring onion for each person. When the rice is cool, mix into it with a fork half a teaspoon of curry powder and all the vegetables.

Serve this salad with cooked meat and lettuce.

Things to do

The choice of a picnic spot is, of course, up to you. Perhaps you have favourite places to which you keep returning. Or perhaps you are more adventurous and always seek fresh woods and pastures new. It's a good idea to combine a visit to a special place – like a country house, castle, zoo or museum – with a picnic. You may be taking your picnic to the beach, river or park. You can even have a very enjoyable picnic in your own garden.

If you are in open country, see if you can find and identify twelve varieties of grasses. A book which will help you is *The Observer's Book of Grasses, Sedges and Rushes* by Rose (Warne).

GAMES

Plate tennis. You need a fairly flat plastic plate, preferably the bendy sort that can't crack. Throw it to each other so it spins through the air. If you have two plates you can see who can throw their plate the furthest or the most accurately to an agreed point.

Shadow tag. This is a game for a really sunny day. You play it just like ordinary tag, with 'He' trying to tag another player who then becomes 'He', but instead of touching the body of the other person, 'He' must touch his or her shadow. You may need an umpire to confirm that the shadow was really tagged.

Malayan football. In Malaya the children play this game with a light basketwork ball, but you can play it with any ball of about 15 centimetres (6 inches) in diameter or larger. The players pass the ball from one to another without touching it with their hands. They may use their heads, shoulders, knees, feet or whatever part of their bodies they wish – but not their hands. Count the number of times the ball is touched on from one person to another and try to see if you can keep it in the air longer the next time. At first you may allow the ball to touch the ground once between each touch, but as you grow more skilful you should keep it in the air all the time.

There are lots more ideas for games suitable for a picnic in *Fun and Games Outdoors* by Jack Cox (Piccolo).

The Country Code

Be sure when you are picnicking in the country that you always observe the Country Code. The basic rule is: enjoy the countryside, but do not hinder the work of the countryman.

You can make sure that you follow this basic rule if you follow this code:

1 Walk on the same side of the road as oncoming traffic.
2 Close all gates unless they are obviously meant to be open.
3 Be careful not to damage hedges, fences or walls; always climb over gates at the hinge end.
4 Avoid damaging crops or grass grown for mowing in any way.
5 Don't disturb sheep or cattle and keep your dog on a lead when you are near any livestock.
6 Pick wild flowers very sparingly and never dig them up or pull them up by their roots.
7 Don't pollute ponds or streams in any way.
8 Don't rob birds' nests.
9 Unless you first get permission, don't light a fire. If you do light one, make sure it is not near dry grass or trees, and make sure it is completely out when you leave.
10 Clear up all your litter before you leave.

Always take a paper carrier with you when you go on a picnic. Use it as a rubbish bin for all paper, plastic, leftover food and so on. Take it home with you and put it straight in the dustbin. It saves a lot of time and energy if you do this and also makes the picnic more civilized!

Living off the land

Here are some ideas for eating the foods that you normally think of as 'weeds'. Of course, you need to know what you are doing when you eat things that are strange to you – you don't want to eat a deadly toadstool! If you are interested you might like to look at a book which tells all about eating wild foods – *Food for Free* by Richard Mabey, published by Collins.

Nettles. If you've ever been stung by a nettle, you may not be very keen on eating them but, in fact, the tender tops of the nettle in the springtime can be eaten instead of spinach. Pick the nettles with gloves on, and boil them in salted water until tender. Presumably you know that if you are stung by a nettle in the summer, you only have to rub a dock leaf on to the place to relieve the sting.

Dandelion. Dandelion leaves can be eaten as salad. It is best if you put a flower pot over the leaves for a few days first to blanch (lighten) and tenderize them. Serve the leaves with a dressing of olive oil and lemon juice.

Elderflowers. In June you can make elderflower 'pancakes'. Pick the flowerheads on their stems. Make a thin pancake batter (*see* page 49). Dip the flowerheads into the batter. Heat some fat in a frying pan and fry the flowerheads for a few moments until the batter is just crisp. Put the 'pancakes' out on a piece of greaseproof paper and sprinkle them with sugar. Pick them up by the stem to eat them.

Things to do indoors

Presents for Father's Day

Father's Day is in mid-June (not always on the same date) – a day to give Father a special day and perhaps a special present.

A buttonhole

You will need a small piece of silver foil and a paper handkerchief. Collect some small flowers or a single flower like a rose or carnation and a few leaves (asparagus fern is very good). Put the flowers together in a pretty little group – not too big, of course! Wrap their stems in a strip from the paper handkerchief and damp this paper very slightly to keep the flowers fresh. Now wrap the stems tightly in the silver foil, to hold them closely together. You could twist a black thread round the stems just to hold the buttonhole more securely.

A screwdriver holder

You can buy three small screwdrivers in different sizes from Woolworth's or a hardware shop. To make the holder, you will need: a piece of dark strong cloth about 25 centimetres by 20 centimetres (10 inches by 8 inches), a piece of woollen cloth slightly smaller and 60 centimetres (24 inches) of strong cotton tape.

Line the strong dark material with the woollen material, by laying the woollen material on the other cloth, turning the edges of the dark cloth over the woollen cloth, and stitching them down firmly.

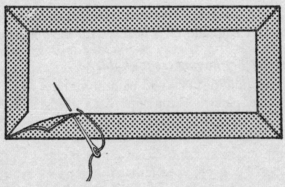

Divide the tape into three pieces of 20 centimetres (8 inches) each. Sew two stretches of tape on to the lining and oversew it at intervals as shown here:

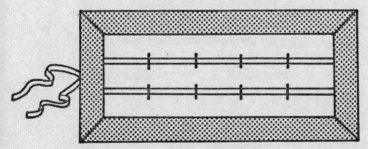

Fold the other piece of tape and sew it at the fold on to one edge of the folder as shown above.

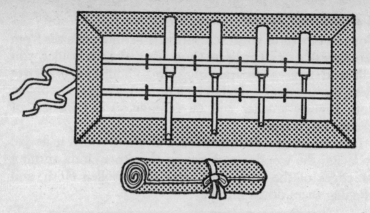

Put the screwdrivers through the slots in the tape. Then roll the folder up and tie it neatly with the outer tape.

Toothpaste or shaving cream holder

Buy a big 'bulldog' clip and paint it all over with enamel paint, making sure that the edges don't stick together by putting a matchstick between them while the paint dries. Fix a tube of toothpaste or shaving cream into the clip. When it is hung up, your father can get the cream out by pressing the tube against the wall.

A pressed-flower picture

Collect simple flowers which can be easily pressed, grasses and ferns. Lay them carefully between pieces of blotting paper or tissue paper between the pages of a heavy book. Put a pile of books on top. You must then leave them for about a week, but you can add further flowers to the pile from time to time.

Arrange the dried flowers into a picture on a piece of coloured card. Don't use too many bits and pieces, as simpler pictures are more effective. Keep your picture inside a border at least 2·5 centimetres (1 inch) wide all round the card. Glue the pieces carefully on to the card and leave them to dry.

Take a piece of cellophane paper the same size as the card and glue it carefully on to the card at the edges. Frame the card with strips of passe-partout, folded over the edges.

Turn the card over. Glue a loop of ribbon at the top to hang your picture by.

Birthday cards

Here are some ideas for cards for summer birthdays.

Potato-cut cards

You need fairly absorbent paper to print on with potato cuts or the paint won't dry quickly and may smudge. You also need a good firm potato, a sharp knife, and coloured ink or poster paints. It is wise to have some newspaper on the table while you are working and a cloth with which you can wipe the paint off the potato from time to time. The size of potato you want will depend on the design you choose, because you only really want one part of the pattern on each potato. Cut the potato in half and cut out the patterns so that they stand out about 1 centimetre (½ inch) above the rest of the surface, like this:

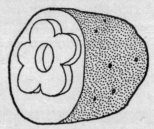

You can make an all-over design, like the first one:
Or a single picture print, like the middle one, to which you can add details with a paint brush, so the card might look like the last one.

Spray-painted pictures

For this sort of decoration you need a piece of netwire with a fine gauge, some poster colours and an old toothbrush.

You will need fairly absorbent paper for the cards and a pattern, such as a leaf or sprig. Lay the leaf carefully on the paper in the position you want it. Hold the netwire about 10 centimetres (4 inches) above the paper, dip the tooth-brush into the paint and rub it across the netwire. The paint will spray through the wire on to the card, leaving a blank silhouette on the sprayed sheet of paper.

Wax pictures

Draw a picture on to a plain piece of paper with a wax crayon. Then paint over the picture with black paint. The wax will not pick up the paint, so the colours will continue to show through.

It happened in June

1215   King John signed Magna Carta, the Great Charter which sets out the liberties of the British people, at Runnymede on 15 June. Some of these liberties are that no man shall be put in prison or banished from the country except according to the law of the land and that there shall be no taxes collected without the consent of what is now Parliament.

1815   The Battle of Waterloo was fought on 18 June, with the British and Prussians on one side against the French, who were defeated under their leader Napoleon.

1870   Charles Dickens, the author of *David Copperfield* and many other books, died on 9 June.

1896   The first modern Olympic Games were held in Athens, where the ancient games had been played.

1919   The first non-stop flight across the Atlantic was made by Alcock and Brown on 14 June.

June birthdays

The zodiac sign for those born between 21 May and 20 June is Gemini – the twins. This is the sign of the artist and the inventor. It is the sign of a versatile, clever, restless and perhaps over-exuberant person. With their double sign, Gemini people tend to have two sides to their character and can surprise people by behaving unexpectedly.

Their birthstone is the pearl or the moonstone. Both these pale stones express youth, beauty, purity and innocence. The moonstone has been described as looking like 'a raindrop seen through a fine mist at early dawn'.

Their lucky day is Saturday; their lucky number is five; their lucky colour is purple or yellow; and their lucky metal is mercury (quicksilver).

Summer

I knew when Summer breathed –
Not by the flowers that wreathed
  The sedge by the water's edge,
    Or gold
    Of the wold,
  Or white and rose of the hedge;
But because, in a wooden box
In the window at Mrs Mock's,
There were white-winged shuttlecocks.
Barbara Euphan Todd

JUNE

My special days this month:

The weather this month:

The coldest day this month was:

The hottest day this month was:

In our park or garden I saw:

My Own Page

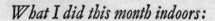

What I did this month indoors:

What I did this month outdoors:

The best/worst thing that happened this month:

Special events in the world this month:

Hot July brings cooling showers,
Strawberries and gilly flowers.

The name of the month

When March was the first month of the year, July was the fifth and was called Quintilis. Then when Julius Caesar reformed the calendar, this month was named after him.

Festivals

1 July is the Canadian National Day.

4 July is Independence Day in the United States of America. This is the day on which the American Declaration of Independence was signed in 1776. It is a major national holiday in the States.

St Swithun's Day is 15 July. St Swithun was a Bishop of Winchester who asked that when he died he should be buried outside his Cathedral in a place where ordinary people would walk over his grave. This was done, but years later, when he was named as a saint, it was decided to take his body into the Cathedral because the monks thought this was more suitable. Legend says that they began the work on 15 July, but it rained that day and for forty days after – so the monks thought better of their plan. They thought St Swithun was angry with them.

There is now a tradition that if it rains on 15 July, it will rain for the following six weeks.

> St Swithun's Day, if thou dost rain,
> For forty days it will remain;
> St Swithun's Day, if thou be fair,
> For forty days it will rain no more.

Watch the weather during the middle of July and see how true this tradition seems to be.

Weather forecasts

> Mackerel sky, mackerel sky,
> Not long wet and not long dry.

A mackerel has ripples of colour on its side; a mackerel sky is a sky with rippled clouds like the side of a mackerel.

When clouds appear like rocks and towers,
The earth's refreshed by frequent showers.

If bees stay at home,
Rain will still come.
If they fly away,
Fine will be the day.

Records

The driest and hottest summer in Britain in the last 250 years was the summer of 1949. If we get a very hot summer, look up the records for that year and see how it compares. (*The Guinness Book of Records* will give you this information.)

Sunrise and sunset

The nights are already beginning to get longer and the days shorter. By the end of July the sun rises at about 5·15 and sets just before nine o'clock. The days are already about an hour shorter than they were on Midsummer Day.

Nature notes

Meadowsweet can be found in shady places now. Smell the flowers which give them their name. The wild rose, the emblem of England, is flowering in the hedgerows in July, alongside the heavy, flat, white blossoms of the elder. If you are lucky you may see a lizard sunning itself on a stone, though it will slip off through the grass or heather as you come near. Pick a sprig of honeysuckle and put it in a small glass of water beside your bed. If you wake up in the middle of the night, its sweet smell will please you.

Things to do outdoors

On the beach

If you are by the seaside, you probably won't need any suggestions about what to do. Nevertheless here are a few ideas to add to your own.

Make a sand castle and dig a moat round it so that the sea will run into the moat when the tide comes in.

Collect pretty stones and shells to make a stone and shell garden on the sand, laying out different 'flower' beds, edged with bits of stick.

Keep some of the prettiest stones and shells you find in a jar of water which will show up their colours. Stones found in shallow water often lose their bright colours when they dry.

Draw out squares on the beach and play hopscotch.

Draw a draughts board on the beach and, with one person using stones and the other shells or pieces of wood, have an enormous game of draughts.

Collect some small, irregular-shaped little stones and play Five Stones. Throw four of the stones down on a flat piece of sand. Throw the fifth one up in the air and see how many of the others you can pick up before you catch the fifth one.

Get a big piece of wood and write your name in huge letters on the sand.

Find a stone or a shell with a hole through it and thread it on a piece of string round your neck like a pendant.

Find some big, flat, smooth stones and take them home. Decorate them with paint to make paperweights and door-stops.

Build a whole sand village with streets, houses, a church, a school, a village shop and so on. Use leafy branches for trees and make little stick figures to people the streets.

Search rock pools for little sea creatures and sea plants. But don't take them out of the pools – it's much more fun to watch them in their natural environment.

Make a giant maze on the beach with a spade or by trampling the paths with your feet. You could play tag in the maze, with no one being allowed to escape by jumping over a 'wall'.

Bury your father under a pile of sand, but make sure you don't get any of it on his face!

Make a pile of soft sand. Put a small stone on the top and gradually cut the sand away, seeing how long you can go on cutting before the stone falls off.

Run races and make an obstacle course along the beach in which you have to jump ditches, run through a trail of sticks or stones, climb under a stick held up by two other forked sticks, and so on.

A spider barometer

Spiders usually make some alteration in their web every twenty-four hours. If these changes are made between six and seven in the evening, they indicate that there will be a clear and pleasant night. If the weather is likely to become rainy, windy or in other ways disagreeable, spiders fix down the ends of the threads of their webs especially short. If these terminating threads are made unusually long, the weather will be calm and is likely to remain so for a week or more. If spiders are completely inactive, it is usually a sign of rain to come. However, if spiders are active during rain,

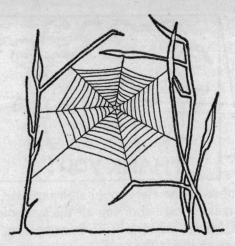

then it is likely that the rain won't last long and will be followed by good weather. These observations are made in William Hone's *Every-day Book* published in 1826. Can you find a spider's web in the garden and see how accurate they are?

Things to do indoors

A present for the teacher

After a year with one teacher, you will now be saying goodbye and going on to another school or another teacher in September. Why not say thank you with a card or small present?

A card

You could adapt one of the cards shown elsewhere in this book into a 'thank you' card, or perhaps you could make a big card from the whole class.

Take a piece of card about 25 by 40 centimetres (10 by 16 inches) which, folded in half, makes a card 25 by 20 centimetres (10 by 8 inches). With the fold at the top, draw a face for each person in your class like a crowd of them gathered in a group.

Every member of the class could sign the card inside. Or you could make a card showing all the symbols of school life: pencils, books, scissors, brushes, compasses, and so on. Write a message inside the card.

Or you could make 'an apple for the teacher'. Take some red or bright-green card about 15 centimetres (6 inches)

square. Fold it so that the fold is along the top. Draw the shape of an apple on it and cut it out, making sure that it remains joined at the top. Fix on some leaves of darker green paper behind the front piece of the card and a little twig for the branch from which the apple came. These can be stuck on with a little piece of Sellotape. Write your message inside.

Presents

BATH-SALT JAR

Buy some bath salts in a packet. Take a clean glass jar with a screw-top lid. With enamel paint, paint a picture on the side of the jar. Paint another picture on the lid, or paint the lid all over in one colour. Let the paint dry well. Fill the jar with bath salts and screw on the lid.

CUFF LINKS

Get two really pretty buttons with a ring-fitting on the back and two smaller, plain buttons with a double hole through the middle.

Link one pretty and one plain button together with strong buttonhole thread and a needle. Using the thread double, start off with a knot in it; pass the needle through the ring-fitting, then through the two holes of the button; pass the thread through the knot so that it holds with the two buttons about $\frac{1}{2}$ centimetre ($\frac{1}{4}$ inch) apart. Now oversew this link to strengthen it by making a loop, passing the needle through it, tightening it round the link. Repeat this oversewing until you have strengthened the whole link. Oversew in one place to hold the thread and cut the end off. Now make the second cuff link in the same way.

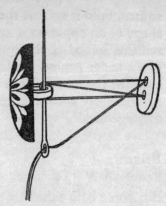

A BOX OF BISCUITS OR SWEETS

Take a box which came to you with biscuits or chocolates in it. Line it neatly with wax paper and fill it with sweets (recipes on pages 33–4) or biscuits. You could fill it with Easter biscuits (page 69) or the shortbread biscuits that follow:

Shortbread biscuits

You will need:

    112 grammes (4 ounces) margarine (or butter)
    200 grammes (7 ounces) plain flour
    56 grammes (2 ounces) castor sugar
    A pinch of salt

If you have no castor sugar, you can put granulated sugar on a pastry board and grind it with a rolling pin to break down the grains. (Or put it in the liquidizer of your mixer, if you have one.)

Mix the sugar and margarine together thoroughly with a wooden spoon. Beat the mixture until it begins to look white and light and the sugar doesn't feel gritty any more.

Mix in the flour gradually. Mix in the salt.

Heat the oven to electricity 350°F, gas Mark 3.

Put the mixture on to a very lightly floured board. Roll it out until it is about 6 millimetres ($\frac{1}{4}$ inch) thick.

With a biscuit cutter or a small glass, cut the mixture into biscuits.

Bake in the oven for 30 minutes.

A BASKET OF FRUIT

Make a basket like the one shown on page 71, but make it in heavier card and larger. Line the bottom with crumpled-up tissue paper and fill with fruit – say, two apples, an orange, a banana and a few cherries.

Or you may like to join together as a class to fill an even larger basket, with each person bringing one piece of fruit.

A PENCIL HOLDER

For this present you will need: a tin, some paint and a bit of Fablon or adhesive felt paper. You can use a baked-bean or soup tin for this, if you have a wall-type tin opener which doesn't leave any jagged edges; otherwise you will need to use a tin which already has a finished edge. Remove the label, clean the tin carefully and dry it well. Paint the *inside* of the tin with enamel. You can buy very small tins at Woolworth's. Don't use too much at a time or it will drip down inside the tin in rivulets. Let it dry thoroughly overnight.

Cut a piece of paper, felt or Fablon which will cover the whole of the outside of the tin, with a small overlap seam. For an ordinary 450-gramme (16-oz) tin you will need a bit 11 by 24 centimetres ($4\frac{1}{2}$ by $9\frac{1}{2}$ inches). If you are covering the tin with non-adhesive paper, you will need to cover the whole of the outside of the tin with a strong glue. Lay the tin on the centre of the paper and then wrap the paper firmly round the tin, sticking down the overlap seam.

You could put a few pencils, a ball point and some felt tip pens into the box.

A summer holiday diary

It's fun to keep a record of the long summer holidays, to look back at through the winter and in the years to come. Buy yourself a scrapbook or make one from sheets of coloured paper in a stiff card cover. Fold the card cover and the sheets of paper. Place the paper sheets inside the cover. Sew them together with nylon wool or strong thread.

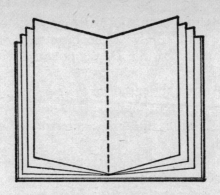

What sort of things might you put in your holiday book? Well, if you are going away, it's easy. Postcards of the places you visit. (You can send the cards to close relatives and ask them to keep them for you, thus killing two birds with one stone, so to speak!) You could put in photographs of the family on holiday; small souvenirs like the label from a bottle from abroad, ticket stubs if you go to a show or cinema, stamps or coins of the country if you go abroad (the coins can be stuck in with Sellotape); pressed flowers and dried grass collected on a picnic; your own drawings of the places you visit or of your own home; bus tickets from journeys you make; programmes of a summer fête or theatre; a map of any trips you take.

Of course, you would write about what you do and see. You could write a poem about a special occasion. You can illustrate your writing with any of the items suggested above, or anything else you may think of.

It happened in July

1588 On 20 July the Spanish Armada arrived off the Lizard (in Cornwall) and joined battle with the English navy between 21 and 28 July, when the Spanish were defeated and their ships scattered.

1789 The Bastille (a prison in Paris) was stormed by the people on 14 July at the beginning of the French Revolution. Bastille Day is now the national day of France.

1817 Jane Austen, the author of *Pride and Prejudice* and other books, died on 18 July.

1873 Bertram Mills, the circus proprietor, was born on 11 August.

1909 Blériot flew the first aeroplane across the English Channel on 25 July.

1969 Neil Armstrong was the first man ever to step on to the moon on 21 July.

July birthdays

If you are born between 21 June and 22 July, you come under the sign of Cancer, the crab. People born under this star are said to be moody and changeable. They enjoy a joke and can be very funny, but they can also cry easily and be rather over-sensitive; they don't like being teased. They are independent people who like a certain amount of solitude.

Your birthstone is the ruby, described as a 'deep drop of the heart's blood of Mother Earth'. The ruby is a precious stone which always symbolizes riches – 'the price of wisdom is above rubies'. It also stands for contentment and courage.

Your lucky day is Thursday; your lucky number is one and your lucky colour is green.

A riddle

Riddle me, riddle me ree,
A little man in a tree;
A stick in his hand,
A stone in his throat,
If you read me this riddle
I'll give you a groat.

A cherry

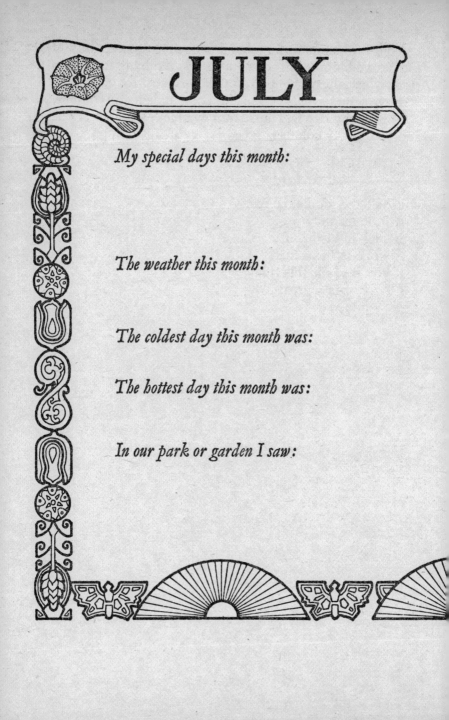

JULY

My special days this month:

The weather this month:

The coldest day this month was:

The hottest day this month was:

In our park or garden I saw:

My Own Page

What I did this month indoors:

What I did this month outdoors:

The best/worst thing that happened this month:

Special events in the world this month:

AUGUST

August brings the sheaves of corn,
Then the harvest home is borne.

The name of the month

This month used to be called Sextilis, the sixth month, and only had 30 days but the Emperor Augustus wanted a month named after himself and he wanted it to be one of the longest, so he stole a day from February which used to have 29 days every year.

Festivals

August Bank Holiday. The long summer holiday in England, Wales and Northern Ireland has now been moved to the last weekend of August. Until 1966 it was the first weekend in August and in Scotland it still is. A Bank Holiday is a day on which banks and therefore most other places of business are closed by law. The other Bank Holidays are:

Christmas Day, Boxing Day, New Year's Day, Good Friday, Easter Monday, the first Monday in May in Scotland and the last Monday in May in other parts of the British Isles. Bank Holidays were started in the days when people did not have a regular annual holiday as they do now.

31 August is the National Day of Trinidad and Tobago.

Weather forecasts

'St Bartholomew brings the cold dew.' St Bartholomew's Day is 24 August. The nights are cooling now. Is the dew really heavier in the mornings on the grass?

Sunrise and sunset

By the end of August sunrise has slipped back to six o'clock and sunset is eight o'clock. The long summer evenings are ending.

Nature notes

This is the month for the harvest. The wheat, oats and barley are ripe in the fields and you may see the great combine harvesters at work. It is also the season for wasps, so watch out for them, particularly near fruit trees. The young birds are learning to fly. Watch them trying out short-distance flights while their confidence grows. The birds are beginning to collect together to fly off for their winter migration to warmer climates. Watch out for the swallows gathering on the telegraph wires and along the roof tops, in great flocks.

Things to do outdoors
Watching meteors

A meteor is a piece of matter from outer space which burns up when it enters the atmosphere of our planet, Earth. Sometimes pieces of these meteors fall to the ground as 'meteorites', like bits of rock or iron. There will probably be some examples of meteorites in your local museum.

On any clear night you can see meteors – 'shooting stars' – flying across the sky. But at certain times of the year you can see them more often than at other times. It is thought that this is when the Earth's path round the sun crosses an area where there is a burnt-out comet, originally a great group of tiny particles which moved together round the sun. The times at which you will see the most shooting stars are 29 July to 18 August, 14–19 November and 8–15 December. See how many meteors you can see during August.

Boule

For this game, which is played very widely in France, you need a small ball about the size of a ping-pong ball called the 'jack', and two regular-sized, fairly heavy balls for each player. You could use tennis balls, but they will bounce too much unless you are very careful. You can buy properly weighted boules in some toyshops. You also need a clear space of flat ground.

One player throws the jack some yards ahead of the starting line. The players then take it in turn to throw their balls towards the jack, trying to get as near it as possible. A second ball may well be used to knock another player's ball away from the jack. When all balls have been thrown, the person with his ball nearest to the jack is the winner.

Fives

This is a very old ball game which was known in the time of Queen Elizabeth I, and was declared by her to be 'the best sport she had ever seen'.

You need a garden wall with a piece of smooth ground in front of it and a tennis ball (or rubber ball of about the same size). Draw a line with chalk on the wall about a yard from the bottom. Mark a long line on the ground about 3 metres (3 yards) from the wall and two lines joining this line at right angles to the wall. This space marks the 'bounds'. The players stand in a row outside the boundary line, players from each team standing alternately.

The first player begins by bouncing the ball on the ground and then batting it against the wall (and above the line) with his hand, so that on its return it bounces outside the bounds. The ball should fall outside the bounds only for the first stroke; after that it must bounce inside the bounds, otherwise the other team gets a point. The players then strike the ball in turn, first one team and then the other. If any player misses the ball on the rebound, hits the wall below the line or hits the ball out of bounds, the other team scores one. The ball is then served again, to bounce outside the bounds. The first team with fifteen points wins.

Flower and leaf chains

Daisy chains

Gather daisies with long stems; make a loop in the stem; put the head of another daisy through it, then tighten up the loop to hold the daisy. Another method is to make a split in the stem of the daisy and put the stem of the next one through it, so that they hold together. Daisy means 'day's eye', because this flower opens when the sun rises, and shuts when the sun sets.

Dandelion stem chains

Gather a great many dandelions and nip off their flowers. The stems are hollow, and one end is smaller than the other. Push the small end into the larger one, and you will have a green ring of any size that you choose. Then put another stem through the ring, like a link in a chain, and join it by pushing the narrow end into the wide one again. Continue until you have made a chain of the length you want, then join the first and last rings with a final ring.

Ivy or beech-leaf chains

Gather leaves with long stems, but don't take too many without first asking if it is all right to do so. Put the stem of one leaf through the top of the other, and pass it back underneath through its own leaf, like this:

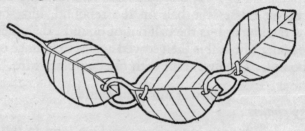

Making a wild-flower collection

Collect just one or two good specimens of each flower that you find, making sure that you have a couple of leaves too, but that you have not harmed the plant or the root. If you suspect that a flower you find might be rare, or rare for the area, *don't* pick it. Identify your flowers from a good book on wild flowers. (I recommend *The Oxford Book of Wild Flowers* by Gregory, *The Concise British Flora in Colour* by Keble Martin and *Flowers of the Field* by Johns. You could borrow these or other books from your library and later, perhaps, ask for one for a birthday present.) Then take the flowers and place them between two sheets of blotting paper in a thick book. Place some heavy books or other weights on top of the book and leave the pile for a week. When the flowers have dried, stick them into a scrap-book, saying what the flower is, when it grows and where and when you found it.

Holiday visits

During the holidays try to make a visit to a local place of interest each week. This will give you something to plan for, something to enjoy, and something to look back on.

Here are some ideas:

Ask a local farmer to let you see round his farm; arrange a visit to your local fire station, factory, police station, water works, sewage works, newspaper, nature reserve or whatever place there is of local interest. You should make arrangements for this sort of visit well in advance and the manager may ask you to make up a small party to go round. Go to your local museum and see what you can find out from it about the area where you live. Take a drawing book and pencil and draw some of the exhibits there. Visit a National Trust property, ancient monument or stately home that is open to the public. You may have to pay to do this; some are very reasonable but others are more expensive and will need to be kept for a special treat. Take a picnic to the seaside, to a well-known beauty spot or to a high site where you will be able to see out across the countryside. Some parks and woodlands now have nature trails which you can follow and learn about the various points of interest. Is there a zoo near where you live, or a bird sanctuary you could visit? If you live near a cathedral town, go and see the cathedral and any other interesting buildings and sites in the town.

These are just a few ideas. I am sure that if you watch, listen and read your local paper you will think of many other visits you could make.

You could keep a holiday scrapbook, in which you write about all the places you visit and stick in any souvenirs you

may have collected (such as tickets, postcards, photographs, your own sketches, and so on).

Things to do indoors

A wormery

Worms are not, you might say, the sort of pet which is likely to be very faithful or even interesting! Faithful, no, but interesting – well, see for yourself.

To make a wormery you need a large glass jar, some garden soil and some worms. Fill your jar with soil and put the worms in on top. Soon they'll disappear and before long you'll see them tunnelling against the side of the glass. Watch for the worm-casts like little hillocks that they will throw up on the surface of the soil. How do they do this? Well, worms eat the earth as they tunnel and cast it out behind them. If you touch the worm-casts you will find that they are made of very powdery, smooth soil, because the worms have broken down and mixed up the earth as it passed through them.

You can try an experiment with your wormery to see how well worms mix up soil, which is why they are so valuable in the garden. This time fill your glass jar with layers of soil which can be easily distinguished: a layer of gravel, a layer of earth, a layer of clay, some sand, another layer of earth and some dry leaves on top. Add a little water. Put a sheet of paper round the glass jar, so that the worms will be in the dark as if they were really underground. Now watch to see what your worms do to the layers of soil during the next few weeks.

When you think your worms have lived in the wormery long enough, be sure to put them back safely in the garden.

A rain gauge

Here is another instrument you can make to help you with your weather observations.

You will need a large bottle – about one pint or one litre in volume. It can be made of either glass or plastic. You will need to cut the top off about one-third down. If you are using a plastic bottle you can do this very carefully with a sharp knife or saw. If you are using a glass bottle, tie a string round at the point where you want the bottle to be cut. Light one end and let the string burn right round the bottle (if you wet the string first with paraffin it will burn faster, but you must ask permission before you use the paraffin). Then douse the bottle in a bucket of cold water and give it a knock. The bottle should break off at the point where the string is, because the contrast between the heat and cold will make it fragile just there. Now you have two parts of the bottle, like this:

On the lower half, using white enamel, paint the measures $\frac{1}{2}$ centimetre, 1 centimetre, $1\frac{1}{2}$ centimetres, etc, up to 6 or 7 centimetres (or if you prefer, $\frac{1}{4}$ inch, $\frac{1}{2}$ inch, $\frac{3}{4}$ inch and one inch, and then the quarters up to two or even three inches). Be sure you take account of the thickness of the bottom of the bottle. Now turn the top of the bottle upside down into the bottom, like a funnel:

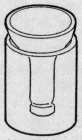

Place your rain gauge in a place where the rain will fall into it without dripping off any tree or building and where it will not be sheltered. Record the rainfall daily.

A noticeboard

Do you have bits and pieces you want to keep and nowhere to display them? Things like postcards, programmes, invitations, pictures of your favourite pop star or motor bike, badges, birthday cards and other souvenirs? Why not make a noticeboard, so that you can keep them all together where you can see them and know where they are when you want them?

You need a piece of strong card or light board and a piece of plain cloth large enough to cover the board and lap over behind it. You also need some narrow black elastic. You can buy this by the metre or yard or on cards, which usually hold about 3 metres (3 yards).

Glue the cloth smoothly over the board, lapping it over the sides and fixing it down behind carefully. You could use an adhesive material like Fablon for this.

Criss-cross lengths of elastic across the board and fix them very firmly down behind. If you are using a light board, drawing pins would be suitable to fix the ends with. If you are using card, then strong staples would be best.

Now you can fix up your notices, cards and so on behind the network of elastic. Always keep a pen or pencil handy on your board so that you can write up any quick notes you want to fix on it.

1704 The Battle of Blenheim (a village in southern Germany) was fought on 2 August, between the French and Bavarians on one side and the British and Austrians on the other. The latter won a great victory, and the English general, the Duke of Marlborough, was given a stately mansion near Woodstock, Oxfordshire, called Blenheim Place in memory of his success. Sir Winston Churchill, a descendant of the Duke, was born there.

1715 Thomas Doggett, an actor, was awarded a prize of a coat and badge for a waterman's race on the Thames – a race which is still rowed annually in London.

1910 Florence Nightingale, the pioneer of modern nursing, known as 'the Lady with the Lamp' by soldiers in the Crimean War hospitals, died on 13 August.

1933 The hottest ever known temperature was recorded in Mexico. It was 136·4° Fahrenheit on 11 August.

1950 Princess Anne was born on 15 August.

August birthdays

Leo, the Lion, is the sign of those born between 23 July and 22 August. People born under this sign are reputed to look rather like lions with a thick mane of hair and an

appearance of laziness. They are supposed to be lazy and energetic in turn, to be proud, happy, enthusiastic and playful. Sometimes they can be very angry and roar like a lion, but they are normally warm and generous.

The birthstone for Leo is the sardonyx, a layered stone of brown and white which is often made into cameo brooches and rings, with a white figure cut out from the brown background. The sardonyx is supposed to give eloquence and married happiness.

The lucky day for Leos is Friday; the lucky number three and the lucky colour gold.

Pied beauty

Glory be to God for dappled things –
   For skies of couple-colour as a brinded cow;
      For rose-moles all in stipple upon trout that swim;
Fresh-firecoal chestnut falls; finches' wings;
   Landscape plotted and pieced–fold, fallow and plough;
      And all trades, their gear and tackle and trim.

All things counter, original, spare, strange;
   Whatever is fickle, freckled (who knows how?)
      With swift, slow; sweet, sour; adazzle, dim;
He fathers-forth whose beauty is past change:
   Praise him.

                    Gerard Manley Hopkins

AUGUST

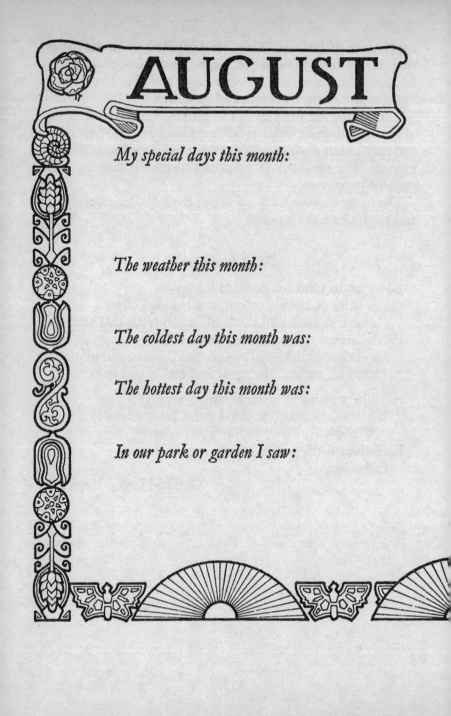

My special days this month:

The weather this month:

The coldest day this month was:

The hottest day this month was:

In our park or garden I saw:

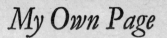

My Own Page

What I did this month indoors:

What I did this month outdoors:

The best/worst thing that happened this month:

Special events in the world this month:

SEPTEMBER

Warm September brings the fruit,
Sportsmen then begin to shoot.

The name of the month

When September was the seventh month it was given the
Latin name for seven, *septem*.

Festivals

Festival of Lanterns (7 September). In Florence in Italy there
is a special festival for children. Each child lights a candle
in a coloured paper lantern and walks through the city
with the lantern hanging from a long cane. In one of the
big squares all the children congregate with their lanterns.
There is singing and dancing and the children go into the
church to be blessed.

Harvest Home (24 September). When all the harvest was
safely home and stored in the barns, there were celebrations
on the farms and services of thanksgiving in the churches.

Harvest home, harvest home,
We have ploughed, we have sowed,
We have reaped, we have mowed,
We have brought home every load.
Hip! hip! hip!
Harvest-home!

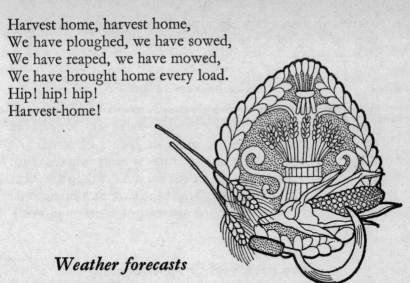

Weather forecasts

And now, let's face
it, winter is on the way. What sort of winter will it be?

Onions' skin, very thin,
Mild winter coming in,
Onions' skin, thick and tough,
Coming winter cold and rough.

Horses', dogs' and cats' coats are said to be especially
thick in preparation for a hard winter.
Any wildfowl seen before October, flying directly south
and very high, means an early and severe winter.

When squirrels eat nuts on the tree,
Winter as warm as warm will be.

Note these and any other sayings your family and friends
can tell you and see if you can correctly forecast how severe
or mild the winter will be.

If the north wind blows on Michaelmas Day,
The month of October is sunny and gay.

If St Michael's Day (29 September) is cold, is it true that you have a good October? The Michaelmas daisies will be flowering now.

The harvest moon

The harvest moon is the great full moon of the autumn equinox (21 September) – when day and night lengths are equal, just before we go into the dark days of winter. At this time of the year the moon's orbit is nearly parallel with the horizon so that the moon rises at almost the same time each evening. Even in a city street the harvest moon can be a very special sight if seen at the end of a street, glowing orange in the sky.

Sunrise and sunset

The dark, longer nights are really drawing in now. By the end of September it is nearly 7 o'clock before the sun rises and it has set before 8 in the evening. So at the Autumn Equinox on 21 September you have the equal hours of darkness and light.

Nature notes

The harvest is over now, with the exception of some of the root crops like sugar beet, and the fields are beginning to be ploughed ready for the winter planting. The vermilion berries of the mountain ash or rowan may be seen in the gardens and streets and growing wild in the Highlands of Scotland.

Many of the summer flowers are gone now, but some remain – the yellow ragwort, the tansy with its aromatic-smelling leaves (bruise one and smell for yourself), the yarrow or Old Man's Pepper and the scarlet pimpernel, known as Poor Man's Weatherglass because it closes up in cloudy weather. Another flower which reacts to the weather is clover, which folds its leaves so that the undersides

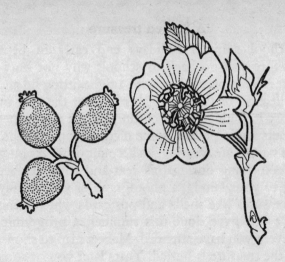

show at dawn, dusk and in wet weather. The wild roses of summer are turning into the scarlet hips of autumn and the hawthorn berries are also reddening in the hedgerows.

Things to do outdoors

Conker base

Conkers may not be quite ready yet, but they will be during the next few weeks; for this game you need a large number, so you'll need to search for them unless, like us, you have your own secret conker tree.

You really need 100 conkers for each player, but you could adjust the rules to the amount you actually have, or put the conkers back in position between each round.

Mark out a big square, say with sides 9 metres (30 feet) long. At each corner place a pile of conkers, at least 20 for each player. The players take it in turn to round the four corners of the square, from 'base' to 'base', picking up 5 conkers at each base, so that at the fourth corner they should be holding 20 conkers in their two hands – quite a feat! See who can pick up the biggest total in 5 turns – 20 is the maximum, which is why you need 100 for each person.

A buried treasure

The school summer holidays end early in September. Just before you go back to school, why not bury a time treasure? Get a plastic box with a tight-fitting lid and put in it a collection of things which represent the year in which you bury it. Things like a cutting from a newspaper about some outstanding event, some pictures showing the sort of clothes people are wearing, an account of what you yourself have been doing during this year and what has been happening to your family, a photograph of your family, some little treasures like shells and postcards which remind you of what you have done this summer, a programme from some event you have attended. Make a map to show exactly where the treasure is buried. Years later you or some other person may dig it up and remember what was happening at this time. We as children buried a time treasure on a rock outcrop in the central provinces of India. I often wonder if anyone has ever found it.

Looking at the Milky Way

At this time of year you can see the Milky Way spreading across the night sky from east to west. The Milky Way is what we call a galaxy – that is, a vast collection of stars grouped very close together.

Look at the Milky Way on a clear night. What can you find out about it from books in the library?

Things to do indoors

Harvest decorations

Perhaps you have a Harvest Festival at school or Sunday school, when everyone brings the fruits of the harvest to be displayed and shared out among the sick and old people. It is also a time when you can decorate the house to remind you of the year's harvest which, if you live in a town, may seem rather distant!

Corn star

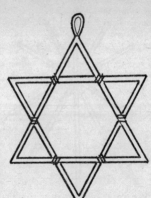

Take corn stalks or drinking straws
and form them into a star, like the
drawing on the left.
Tie the joins with red cotton and
hang the star from a loop.

A lighter corn star

Make a star from smaller
pieces of corn or a packet of
spills, by weaving them
together at the centre, like
the drawing opposite.

Then cut off the edges with a razor blade to finish off the
star shape. Hang a loop of thread from one edge to hang the
star from.

Another straw star

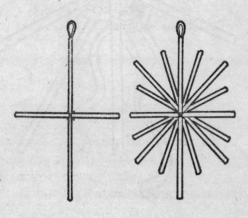

Take two corn stalks
or straws and tie them
together across one
another, like the first
drawing on the right.
Then add more and
more straws until you
get a star shape, like
the second drawing on
the right.

A fourth straw star

Take three corn
stalks or straws and
tie them with red
thread into a cross,
like the drawing
opposite.
Add two further
straws, like the
drawing on the far
right.

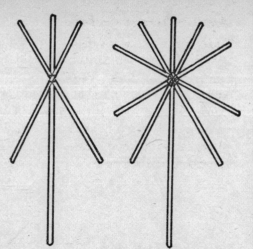

Now take a piece of narrow red ribbon and weave it in and out
through the spokes of the star, like the drawing below left.

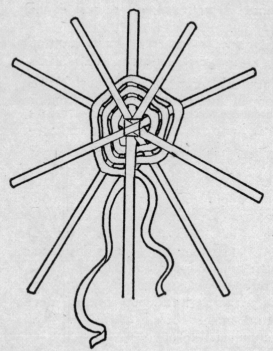

Join the ribbon so
that the ends hang
down behind the
spokes of the star.
Tie a thread to the
top spoke so that
you can hang it up.

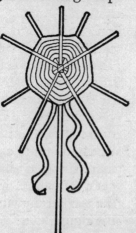

Another harvest symbol

Take three straws of equal length. Form them into a triangle, tying them together where the straws meet and cross. Form a loop at the top to hang it from. Tie an ear of wheat so it hangs from the tip of the triangle.

A football scarf

Can you knit? If so, the easiest thing you can make is a scarf in the colours of your brother's or father's football team (or in your school or club colours, or just in the colours you like!).

You will need 85 grammes (3 ounces) of double knitting wool in one colour, the same in a contrasting colour and a pair of number 8 needles. Cast on 30–40 stitches, depending on the width you want, in the darker shade. Knit 20 rows in plain knitting. Then change to the lighter colour and knit another 20 rows. Change back to the first colour and continue knitting 20 rows of each colour until the scarf has reached its desired length. You should have about 14 grammes ($\frac{1}{2}$ ounce) of each of the wools left over for the fringe. Finish with 20 rows of the darker colour and cast off.

Now make a fringe for your scarf. Take a piece of card about the size of a playing card. Wrap wool round the length of the card ten times. Cut along one edge, holding the strands together at the other edge. Take the strands and push the folded end through one edge of the scarf to form a loop. Pass the cut ends through the loop and pull them down to form a tassel. A crochet hook is useful when you are doing this, to pull the wool through.

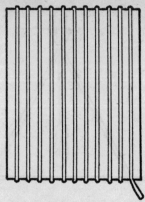

Make tassels like this in alternating colours along both ends of the scarf.

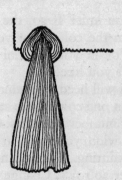

A seed collage

There are seeds and seed pods on many plants at this time of year and there are other seeds which you can collect in your own kitchen. Collect together a selection in an egg box, using the sections to separate each kind.

You can collect garden seeds and household ones like lentils, dried peas, butter beans, dried orange and apple pips, melon seeds (dry them off in the oven, so they go stripey brown), rice and barley.

Take a piece of dark-coloured card. Mark on it the outline of the picture you want to make. Choose a fairly simple shape, like an animal or a house, at the beginning, and move on to more complicated shapes as you see how it goes.

You will need some quick-drying glue such as Uhu or Bostik, a spatula for spreading it on the paper, tweezers to pick up the seeds, some clear varnish and a brush to spread it with (nail varnish would do or you can buy varnish at the paint counter in Woolworth's). Put glue on only a small bit of your picture at a time. Put the chosen seeds on to the patch very closely together with the tweezers. Glue another patch and continue until you have covered the whole picture. Allow the glue to dry completely.

Then spread the varnish very thinly over the seeds. Make sure you varnish the sides of the seeds as well as the tops. Try not to let the varnish run over the edge of the seed picture on to the surrounding card. Let the varnish dry before you stand the picture up.

A bowl of bulbs

If you want to have bulbs ready to give as presents at Christmas, you must start thinking about hyacinths in September, though narcissi can be grown to flowering point in about 5 weeks, so you needn't plant them until mid-November.

Choose a pretty bowl. You can buy plastic ones quite cheaply, or look out for a suitable china one at jumble sales or on junk stalls. Fill it with pebbles, which you have washed well first. Gravel can also be used. Add a few small pieces of charcoal to keep the water fresh. Place your bulbs on top, making sure they don't touch each other. Add water so it just touches the underside of the bulbs. Put the bulbs in a warm room and check to see that they always have enough water.

You can also grow bulbs in bulb fibre which you buy in a gardening shop in the autumn. You will have to start them off in a dark cupboard. There will be instructions on the packet of fibre which, if followed, will give the best results.

You may like to put a broad ribbon and bow round the base of a plastic flower pot to make it look prettier, but if you have found a pretty bowl for your bulbs, you won't need this.

It happened in September

1533 Queen Elizabeth I was born on 7 September.
1666 The Great Fire of London raged from 2 to 6 September.
1825 The first railway line in the world, the Stockton and Darlington colliery line, was opened on 27 September.
1939 Britain declared war on Germany on 3 September. The Second World War lasted until August 1945.

September birthdays

Those born between 23 August and 22 September come under the sign of Virgo – the young girl. People born under this sign are said to be quiet and methodical, efficient and well-behaved at school. Although they are adaptable, they don't like other people using their things and they can be fussy about their food. They love small pets and they try hard to please the people about them.

Born in September, your birthstone is the deep-blue sapphire. This stone, the colour of the sky, represents the good and the poor. It is supposed to protect people against sadness.

Your lucky colour is black; your lucky number seven; and your lucky day Tuesday.

September

Now every day the bracken browner grows,
 Even the purple stars
 Of clematis, that shone about the bars,
Grow browner; and the little autumn rose
 Dons, for her rosy gown,
 Sad weeds of brown.

Now falls the eve; and ere the morning sun,
 Many a flower her sweet life will have lost,
 Slain by the bitter frost,
Who slays butterflies also, one by one,
 The tiny beasts
 That go about their business and their feasts.

Mary Coleridge

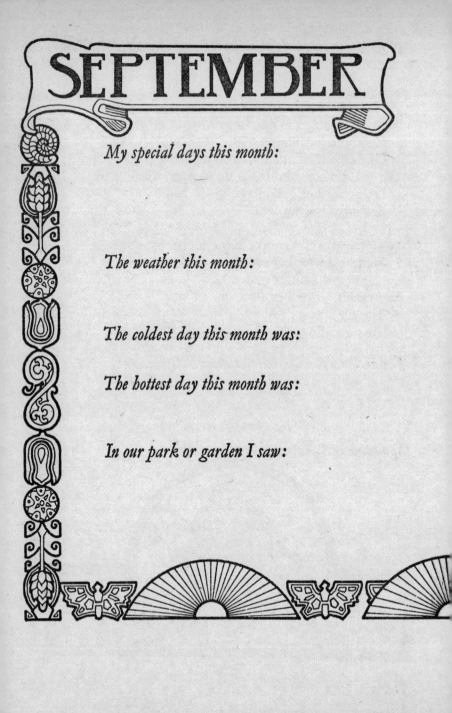

SEPTEMBER

My special days this month:

The weather this month:

The coldest day this month was:

The hottest day this month was:

In our park or garden I saw:

My Own Page

What I did this month indoors:

What I did this month outdoors:

The best/worst thing that happened this month:

Special events in the world this month:

OCTOBER

Fresh October brings the pheasant,
Then to gather nuts is pleasant.

The name of the month

October stands for the eighth month, from the Latin 'octo', meaning eight. When March was the first month of the year, October was the eighth.

Festivals

1 October is the National Day of Nigeria and of China.

Hallowe'en (31 October) – the night of witches, goblins and ghosts, the night of magic.

When I was a child in Canada, Hallowe'en rather than Guy Fawkes was the autumn occasion. We all dressed up in fancy dress and went from house to house asking the inhabitants to 'shell out'. And out they came with sweets, fruit and nuts which we stored greedily into the bags we'd brought along.

Originally this custom must have been to 'buy off' witches and hobgoblins and to some extent we were still being 'bought off', because if anyone refused to 'shell out' nasty boys would do nasty things to them like painting their windows and spooking them.

It was like a cross between 'a penny for the Guy' and carol singing, for we showed off our clothes to the 'shellers out'.

Weather forecasts

'A hard winter follows a fine St Denis's Day' (9 October). See how true it is that a hard winter follows if the first part of October is fair.

'Fifteen fine days hath October.' Is this true?

Sunrise and sunset

By the end of October it is almost 8 o'clock before the sun rises and it is dark before 6 o'clock in the evening. But on the fourth Sunday in October we change back from summer time to Greenwich Mean Time, so that the winter evenings are darker and the dawns are earlier.

Nature notes

October was described by John Keats as 'Season of mists and mellow fruitfulness'. The leaves are changing colour on the trees with the early frosts. The sugar beet and other root crops are now being harvested. Next year's wheat will be sown in the newly ploughed fields. There are varieties of mushrooms and toadstools in the fields and woods. See 'Living off the Land' in the May chapter for details of which mushrooms and toadstools you **shouldn't** eat, and remember, **never** eat any unidentified fungus.

Things to do outdoors

Autumn leaves

One Autumn we went to the park and collected all the autumn leaves we could carry home. The best specimens we kept aside and pressed particularly carefully, and from them we made a book of leaves with the names of the trees and examples of their leaves and seed pods.

The others we pressed too, though with less precision, and then, when they were dry, we decorated a whole wall in my daughter's bedroom with them in a great sweeping pattern. They were fixed to the wall with Sellotape, but this was a mistake. When we took them down the emulsion paint came down too. It is better to use Blu-tak, which holds firmly and leaves no trace.

Press the leaves by placing them between the pages of books and putting heavy books on top. Leave the pile of books for a week or more, so that the leaves dry and flatten. The colour from the leaves can mark the pages of the books, so put paper handkerchiefs or tissue paper between the leaves and the pages.

Find out why leaves change colour in the autumn and fall from the trees. The timing depends on the weather before

(has it been wet or dry?) and the weather now (is it cold and windy or mild?).

Conkers

Collect chestnuts as they fall to the ground from the horse chestnut trees. Bore a hole through the centre very carefully with a skewer. Thread a string through the hole and knot one end so that the conker will not slide off. Now your conker is ready.

Take it in turns with your friend to be the 'challenger' and the 'challenged'. The challenged conker is held so it sways gently on the end of its string and the challenger whacks down on it, trying to crack or smash it. Then the challenged conker becomes the challenger.

If you break the other person's conker, your own takes over its 'life' and becomes a 'twoer'. If a twoer is smashed, the conqueror takes over both lives and becomes a 'three-er'.

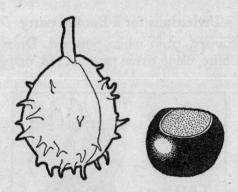

And of course, if a three-er smashes a 'sixer', it becomes a 'niner'. My son had a very vicious and wizened little conker which was at least a 'two-hundred-and-fiftier', having survived one season and returned to battle the next year!

Autumn

I knew when Autumn came –
Not by the crimson flame
  Of leaves that lapped the eaves
    Or mist
    In amethyst
  And opal-tinted weaves;
But because there were alley-taws*
(Punctual as hips and haws)
On the counter at Mrs Shaw's.

Barbara Euphan Todd

Things to do indoors

Hallowe'en is the great occasion for October parties. But you must remember that Guy Fawkes Night is coming up early in November, and make your invitations for your Bonfire Night party in good time.

Invitations for a Bonfire party

Take an ordinary, plain white postcard. Draw on it the logs of a bonfire, using tissue paper in red, orange and yel-

low to show the flames of the bonfire. Write the message with a felt tip pen.

* An alley-taw was a marble.

Hallowe'en party

Invitations

Using a double card of deep orange, draw and cut out the shape of a pumpkin, so that the card remains joined at the top or side. Cut out the shape of the eyes, nose and mouth

on the front piece of the card. Stick pieces of yellow tissue paper behind these holes, so that they look as if they are lit up by a candle inside. Write your message on the back bit of the card.

A Hallowe'en (or Guy Fawkes) mask

With these two occasions so close together, here are some masks for you to make, either for a Hallowe'en party or for your Guy on Bonfire Night.

Paper masks

You need a piece of thin card about 20 by 25 centimetres (8 inches by 10 inches). Cut a shape out of it like this:

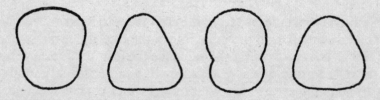

Hold the shape over your face to mark the eyes carefully in position with a pencil. It's best if someone can help you do this. Cut out the eyes.

Cut out ears from the card, making them quite big, like this:

Paste the ears on behind the face, bending over the edges so that they stand away from the head.

You can add further features like whiskers for a rat, a mane for a lion with a fringe of paper, eye-lashes of paper for a monkey or human.

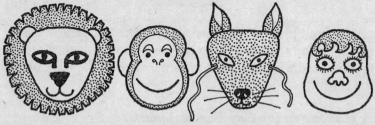

Stick some Sellotape on the side of the mask near your ears to strengthen it. Punch holes through the Sellotape and tie on bits of string with which to tie the mask round your head.

A papiermâché mask

You will need a good big lump of Plasticine or clay with which to model the face and then lots of newspaper strips and some cold-water paste to make the mask from your model.

First model the face from the clay. It is easiest to do it on a board lying flat on the table. Make the face about the same size as yours – or bigger – and make the features as exaggerated and grotesque as you can, with a big nose and mouth and bulging eyes. Smear your model with a coat of Vaseline,

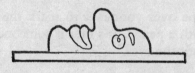

so that you will be able to strip off the dried mask when it is ready. Paste on about 6 layers of paper with cold-water paste and leave it to dry. Remove the dried mask from the clay, patching up any thin places or places which come adrift when you move it. The surface will be rather rough and will need sand-papering to make it smooth. Then paint the mask over first with a layer of flat white paint. Cut holes for the eyes (which can be either a little larger than a nail-point or the size of your own eyes), for the nostrils and mouth, and holes at the side above the ear for a string or elastic to hold the mask on. Now paint your mask as vividly and horrifically as possible. Add cotton wool or frilled paper for eyebrows, moustache or beard to suit the character you are representing.

Jack o' lantern

Make a spooky lantern to stand in your window on Hallowe'en. Get a pumpkin or a very large swede or turnip. Cut off the top and put it aside. Hollow out the inside of the pumpkin as much as possible. Cut eyes, a nose and a mouth with jagged teeth right through the outside. Fix a candle firmly inside. Light it. Put on the 'lid', the piece which you cut off the top. Stand the jack o' lantern on your window sill, so that it looks out into the dark night.

You can also make smaller lanterns using scooped out oranges and following exactly the same method.

Fancy dress for a Hallowe'en party

With a bit of ingenuity you can turn everyday clothes into exotic fancy dress, though it's fun if you have a dressing-up box with articles collected from friends and relatives and from jumble sales. We used to have some trailing dresses, and one particularly beloved, skin-tight, shiny silk one, fur jackets bought for a few pence at jumble sales, big floppy hats and a collection of old scarves, bits of net and cloth flowers to decorate the hats and dresses with.

A PIRATE

You need jeans or trousers tucked into gum boots (which have the tops turned down), and a white shirt with a brightly coloured scarf or strip of cloth tied nonchalantly round the waist. Tie a loop of thread to a brass curtain ring and hang the loop over your ear so that the ring hangs down just below your ear lobe like an ear-ring. Make a black patch to tie over one eye with a piece of card and some string. Make a hat from black (or black-painted) card. Cut a large circle,

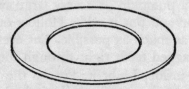

with a smaller circle cut out from the centre just the right size to fit over your head. Take a strip of paper long enough to go round your head with a 5-centimetre (2-inch) overlap,

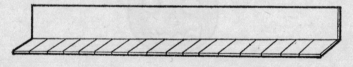

and 15 centimetres (6 inches) deep. Score a line 2·5 centimetres (1 inch) in from one edge. Cut slits into this scored line at 5-centimetre (2-inch) intervals. Join the card in a circle with staples, Sellotape or strong glue.

Slip the circle through the brim of your hat and use the flaps to fix the crown of the hat on to the brim. Bend up one edge of the hat to give a buccaneer touch.

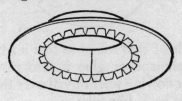

Tie a scarf rakishly round the brim.

Make a sword from a long and a short piece of wood lashed together like this:

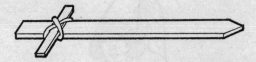

Paint a fierce black moustache on your upper lip with eyebrow pencil or poster paint.

You need a long, flowing gown like a nightgown and a hat made from a quarter-circle of card, like this:

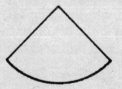

Roll the circle of card round so that it forms a big cone, then staple, Sellotape or glue it into place. Fix a long chiffon or other flowing scarf or veil over the top, so that it hangs down the back, like this:

KINGS AND QUEENS

Here the important things are a cloak and a crown. A cloak can be made from a piece of cloth, an old velvet curtain or a light, brightly coloured blanket. Fix it at the shoulder with a big safety pin made into a brooch with a crêpe-paper rosette (*see* page 51). A crown can be made from a strip of card large enough to go round the head with a 5-centimetre (2-inch) overlap. Draw and cut out the required outline and decorate with painted or gummed paper 'jewels'. The king can wear a belted shirt as a tunic over trousers; the queen a long dress and some necklaces and other jewellery.

Hallowe'en games

The apple harvest is now in and many of the traditional games for Hallowe'en use apples.

LOVERS

A girl puts an apple pip on each cheek. She names them after her two favourite boys, and says:

Pippin, pippin, I stick you there,
He who is true you may declare.

The one which falls off first will be the one who lets her down first.

Pare the skin off an apple or peel an orange in one continuous strip. Throw it with your right hand over your left shoulder. The letter it forms when it lands on the ground is the initial letter of the name of your future husband or wife. There was an old verse which was recited when this was done on 28 October:

St Simon and St Jude, on you I intrude,
By this paring I hold to discover,
Without any delay tell me this day,
The first letter of my own true lover.

BOBBING FOR APPLES

Fill a big bowl with water and place it on a large plastic sheet on the floor. Contestants kneel down and have to get the apples out of the water, using their teeth only. They should keep their hands behind their backs.

Alternatively, stretch a piece of string across the room and hang the apples on lengths of string attached to it. With hands behind their backs, the contestants have to get an apple down with their teeth. Hang the apples on different lengths of string to suit the different heights of the people!

THE GHOULS' STORY

Someone tells a story while the others sit round blindfolded or in a very dark room. At suitable points in the story-teller's narrative an assistant passes round items to illustrate the story. The listeners touch them with horror and screams. You'd better not play this game with people who are too young and sensitive!

Here is a sample story:

Once upon a time a terrible ogre lived in the depths of an evil forest. He used to lie in wait for unsuspecting victims to come to him along the forest paths. (Helper draws a damp leafy branch across the listeners' foreheads.) When he captured anyone he cut them up and ate them. He particularly liked the eyes, which he found most tasty. (Helper puts a peeled grape into the hands or mouths of the listeners.)

Then he liked the flesh from the tender parts. (Helper passes round a bowl with a smooth, warm, damp cloth in it.) And lastly, he enjoyed his victim's guts – he always finished his meal off with these. (Helper passes round a bowl of warm, cooked spaghetti or macaroni.)

But eventually, of course, as always happens to terrible ogres, a dashing and handsome prince came storming in. (Helper rushes round the circle, a cloak flapping in the listeners' faces.) With his trusty sword he cut off the ogre's head and bore it out of the forest dripping with blood. (Helper splashes warm water on the listeners' faces.) And that was the end of that.

Guy Fawkes or Hallowe'en food

TOFFEE APPLES

Get 6 good eating apples and skewer them on strong sticks 10 centimetres (4 inches) long. Put them on a baking tray ready for the toffee.

For the toffee mixture,
you will need:

$\frac{1}{2}$ kilogram (1 lb) sugar;
0·2 litre ($\frac{1}{3}$ pint) water;
1 teaspoon lemon juice.

Boil the sugar and the water together in a saucepan until the mixture is brittle when a little is dropped into a cup of cold water. Add the lemon juice. Dip the apples into the mixture and turn them round and round until they are covered with the toffee mixture. Be extremely careful, because toffee made like this is VERY hot! As hot toffee could give you a nasty burn, it might be better to make it with an adult's help.

BAKED POTATOES

Baking potatoes in a bonfire can be very frustrating – if the potatoes don't get lost in the ashes, they always seem to take far too long to cook and you want to eat them long, long before they are ready. The answer to this problem is to cheat! Cook them in the safety of your own oven first and then just heat them up in the bonfire so that they have the genuine bonfire taste, which it is a pity to lose.

Try to get potatoes that are more or less the same size. Wash them well. Put a little oil on them and rub it all over, then sprinkle salt over the oil. Put the potatoes on a baking tray in the oven and bake for 1–2 hours, depending on the size of your potatoes, in a hot oven at electricity 425°F or gas Mark 6–7

SAUSAGES ON STICKS

Prepare some long, green sticks with sharp, pointed ends. The sticks should be about a metre (3 feet) long and the pointed end should be about 6 centimetres (2 inches).

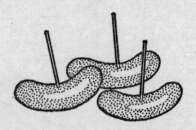

Spear the sausages, pork, beef or frankfurters, on the sticks and cook them over a bonfire. Eat them in buttered rolls with mustard and/or tomato sauce.

It happened in October

1066 William the Conqueror defeated King Harold at the Battle of Hastings on 14 October.

1415 The Battle of Agincourt was fought on 25 October, between the English under King Henry V and the French.

1492 On 12 October Christopher Columbus reached what he thought was India, but it was in fact a Caribbean island; he thus became the discoverer of America.

1632 Sir Christopher Wren, the architect of St Paul's Cathedral in London, was born on 20 October at East Knoyle in Wiltshire.

1805 The Battle of Trafalgar, between the British and the French, was fought on 21 October; it was won by the British, although their Admiral, Lord Nelson, was killed. Trafalgar Day is still celebrated with naval processions.

1863 The English Football Association was founded on 26 October.

1914 Thor Heyerdahl, the Norwegian writer who wrote *The Kon-Tiki Expedition*, was born on 6 October.

October birthdays

If you are born between 23 September and 22 October, you live under the sign of Libra, the balance or scales. Your character is said to have balancing sides. You are talkative, but you are also a good listener. You like people, but you hate crowds. You are up-and-down like an old-fashioned scales – active one moment and then needing to rest and recover. You love beauty and you like writing about what you see and hear.

Your birthstone is the opal. The opal has a reputation for bad luck, except to those whose birthstone it really is. This idea apparently dates from the days of the Black Death in the fourteenth century. People thought that an opal looked bright until its wearer died, and then it lost its shine. For this reason some people thought that the opal actually caused the death. Nowadays it is supposed to represent hope.

Your lucky number is nine; your lucky colour is blue, and your lucky day is Wednesday.

The Hag

The Hag is astride,
  This night for to ride;
The Devil and she together:
  Through thick, and through thin,
  Now out, and then in,
Though ne'er so foul be the weather.

A thorn or a burr
  She takes for a spur:
With a lash of a bramble she rides now
  Through brakes and through briars
  O'er ditches and mires,
She follows the Spirit that guides now.

No beast, for his food,
  Dares now range the wood;
But hushed in his lair he lies lurking:
  While mischiefs, by these,
  On land and on seas,
At noon of night are a-working.

The storm will arise,
    And trouble the skies;
This night, and more for the wonder
    The ghost from the tomb
    Affrighted shall come
Called out by the clap of thunder.
                    Robert Herrick

OCTOBER

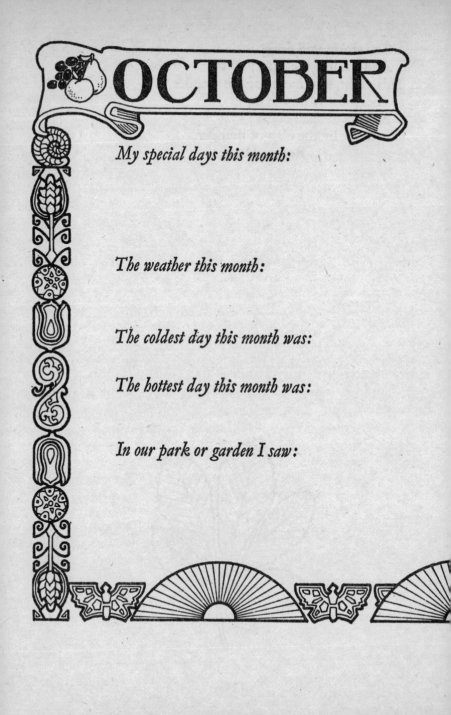

My special days this month:

The weather this month:

The coldest day this month was:

The hottest day this month was:

In our park or garden I saw:

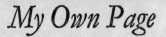

My Own Page

What I did this month indoors:

What I did this month outdoors:

The best/worst thing that happened this month:

Special events in the world this month:

NOVEMBER

Dull November brings the blast,
Then the leaves are falling fast.

The name of the month

November stands for the ninth month, which it was in the old Roman calendar when March was the first month (the Latin for 'nine' is *novem*).

Festivals

Guy Fawkes' Day (5 November). On 5 November 1605 Guy Fawkes tried to blow up King James I and his Parliament. But the plot was discovered and so every year thereafter the anniversary of his failure has been celebrated. Fireworks and bonfires and the burning of 'Guys' go on in every town and village. In Lewes and Rye in Sussex the bonfires and processions are the great celebrations of the year, occasions which are planned for and worked towards for months before.

Please to remember the fifth of November,
Gunpowder treason and plot.
I see no reason why gunpowder treason
Should ever be forgot.

174

7 November is the national day of Russia.
30 November is St Andrew's Day, the patron saint of Scotland.

Weather forecast

St Martin's Day is 11 November, and tradition says: 'If the ice on St Martin's Day will bear a duck, there will be none that will bear a goose all winter.'

Sunrise and sunset

By late November the sun does not rise until after half past seven and it is dark by four o'clock. And if November is a grey and rainy month, it seems as if the hours of daylight are even fewer than they are.

Nature notes

Watch out for the scarlet holly berries in the hedges and gardens. People say that a heavy crop of berries foretells a hard winter. See if you agree.

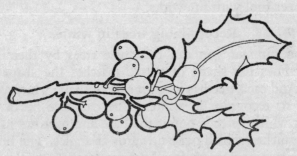

Listen for the tawny owl's 'tu-whit, tu-whoo' at night. The ghostly sound will make you glad you're safe in bed!

November is often the gloomiest month of the year, with lead-grey skies, fogs, rain and gusts of wind which grab the last few leaves from the trees. By the end of the month the gardens look desolate. The few flowers which survive, like chrysanthemums, look dirty and bedraggled from rain. But remember that the remaining blackberries in the hedgerows have their finest flavour now.

Things to do outdoors

The firework code

When you are having your bonfire or firework party, remember these rules and be careful.

1 Keep fireworks in a closed box; take them out one at a time and put the lid back on at once.
2 Follow the instructions on each firework carefully; read them by torchlight, never by a naked flame.
3 Light fireworks at arm's length – preferably with a safety lighter or fuse wick.
4 Stand well back.
5 Never return to a firework once lit – it may go off in your face.
6 Never throw fireworks.
7 Never put fireworks in your pocket.
8 Keep pets indoors.
9 Never fool with fireworks.

Recognizing trees in winter

In the summer you can recognize trees by their leaves. Sometimes the shape of a tree matches the shape of its leaf. And each tree has its own special shape which you can learn to recognize in winter. The oak tree has a sturdy trunk which spreads out at the base and narrows in under the branches, which twist upwards at angles. The branches of the sycamore grow in a V-shape from its trunk, so that the whole tree is rather like a Y. The ash tree has a trunk rather like the oak, but its branches grow straighter and point upwards. The willow, of course, has branches which droop down towards the ground.

Make your own observations about the trees in your neighbourhood so that you can recognize trees without their foliage. To help you recognize them, the following books are useful: *The Ladybird Book of Trees* by Fitzgerald and Vesey (Ladybird); *Your Book of Trees* by M. Hadfield (Faber); *The Observer's Book of Trees* by W. J. Stokoe (Warne).

Things to do indoors

Parkins

In Leeds Guy Fawkes' Day is Parkin Day too – parkins are the traditional food eaten on that day. Here is a recipe for parkin from a book published in 1833.

You will need:
   225 grammes ($\frac{1}{2}$ pound) butter
   1 kilogram (2 pounds) oatmeal
   225 grammes ($\frac{1}{2}$ pound) sugar
   28 grammes (1 ounce) ground ginger
   225 grammes ($\frac{1}{2}$ pound) treacle

Rub the butter into the oatmeal. Mix in the sugar and ground ginger. Stir in the treacle so it will make the mixture into a thick paste. Roll it out into cakes about 1 centimetre ($\frac{1}{2}$ inch) thick, lay them on buttered tins and bake them in a moderate oven (300°F or Mark 2) for about 45 minutes.

Making Christmas cards

With Guy Fawkes' Day and its bonfires and fireworks over in the first week of the month, Christmas begins to loom. If you have friends overseas, you should already be beginning to send off your Christmas cards. So they had better be made now!

From very ancient times people have exchanged small charms or tokens of good luck on various occasions of the year, but it was only in the mid-nineteenth century that the custom of sending Christmas cards started. The history of Valentine cards goes back a century further, when intricate lacy confections were sent by young lovers. In London in 1821 the Post Office delivered about 200,000 extra letters on St Valentine's Day! Of course, the greeting-card business is now enormous, but there is still something very special about the home-made card, both because it is very pleasant to receive and because making it is great fun. Here are some ideas for Christmas cards, which may lead you on to many more inventions of your own.

With Christmas cards you are likely to be wanting to send out a number at a time to your friends and relations. You can make them all different, for instance by painting pictures, but you may want to make a number using variations on a method. You will need white or coloured card to cut and fold, like this:

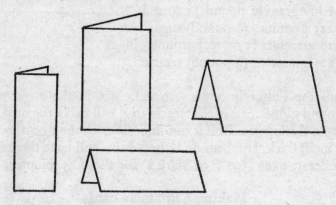

Make sure that the size you have chosen fits a standard-sized envelope or you will find your cards very difficult to send.

Cut-out shapes

Make patterns in stiffish card of the shapes you want to use – star, Christmas-tree ball, bell, candle, Christmas tree. Use these shapes as patterns to cut out shapes from coloured paper. The sort that is gummed on the back is the easiest to use. Stick the shapes on your card with a greeting ('Merry Christmas!') and a message inside.

Put a little glue on the cut-out shape and sprinkle some glitter on it. Let it dry and then shake off the extra glitter on to a piece of paper, so that you can use it again.

Snowflake cards

For these it is best to use a dark-coloured card. Take a piece of thin white paper. Cut it into small squares and circles, not more than about 5 centimetres (2 inches) across. Fold the shape in half, then in quarters, then in eighths:

Cut shapes out across the folds, at the centre and at the edge, being careful not to cut out too much, or too little. A few experiments will show you the best way to do this.

Open out the snowflake and flatten it out. Paste your snow-flakes, of different sizes and shapes, on to your card.

Mosaic cards

On a folded card, build up a picture from scraps of coloured paper which can be both torn and cut with scissors. A snow scene with roughly torn, falling snowflakes can be especially effective, or torn shapes can appear as flowers on a green field.

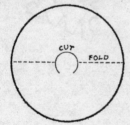

Cut-out cards

Fold your card at the top. Draw and colour a figure on it, including the folded edge in the picture. Cut out your picture. Put some glue on the card and sprinkle glitter on it, or add a cotton-wool beard for a Father Christmas figure.

A stand-up card

Using a compass, draw two circles, one inside the other, like this:

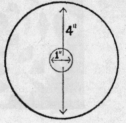

Cut out a shape like this, cutting down round the smaller circle too.

Draw and colour a face on the small circle; draw hands and clothes on the body; write 'Stick together here', as shown.

STICK TOGETHER HERE   STICK TOGETHER HERE

This is how the card will look when it is stuck together and stood up on someone's shelf.

'Stained-glass' card

Using dark-coloured card, not thick or stiff in texture, fold it at the side. Draw and cut out shapes in the middle of the front half in the design you want; use scissors with sharp points to avoid bending the card when you cut out the shapes. Start with simple designs and go on to more complex ones as you increase your skill. Paste scraps of coloured tissue or cellophane paper over the holes from the inside of the card.

You could make a card like this from a single unfolded piece of card so that it can be Sellotaped to a window with the light shining through it like a real stained-glass window.

Present-making

You may have been gathering and making presents throughout the year and by now have a dried-flower picture for your mother, a football scarf for your brother and a bowl of bulbs for your aunt. But now is the time to start making all the Christmas presents you have not yet prepared. Here are some further ideas.

A pomander

According to the dictionary, a pomander is a mixture of aromatic substances, usually made into a ball, to be carried about with one, especially as a safeguard against infection. These aromatic substances were sometimes carried in a hollow ball of gold, silver or ivory. Our pomander isn't made of gold, but of an orange. It isn't intended to ward off the plague either, but to make a sweet smell in a clothes cupboard and possibly to ward off moths!

Cardinal Wolsey (1475–1530) is described as entering a crowded room 'holding in his hand a very fair orange, from which the meat or substance within was taken out, and filled up again with parts of a sponge, wherein was vinegar and other confections against the pestilent airs'.

Use thin-skinned oranges and whole cloves to make your pomander. You can buy cloves quite cheaply from a grocer's shop or from some chemists'; they come in little boxes, which will be enough for 2 or 3 pomanders. Be sure you get whole cloves and not the powdered variety.

Stick the cloves very closely together into the orange. When it is completely covered, wrap it in tissue paper and put it away for a few weeks to dry off. If you want to make a pomander that can be hung up, leave two lines between the cloves right round the orange. When the pomander has dried, tie two pieces of ribbon round the pomander, leaving the ends to be tied in a bow or a loop on top, so that it can be hung up.

An oven glove

To make an oven glove in felt you will need two pieces of thick felt about 20 by 30 centimetres (8 by 12 inches) and two pieces of cloth to line the glove. If you can't afford felt, you could use any thick woollen cloth, but you will have to be more careful with the seams or they will unravel. Lay your right hand on a piece of paper the same size as the cloth with your thumb out, like this:

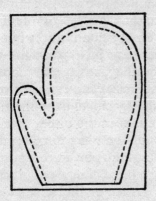

If the person you are giving the glove to is left-handed, make the pattern with your left hand.

Draw a pattern round your hand, making it large enough for the glove to be slipped on and off easily after the seams have been made.

Use this paper pattern to cut out two pieces of felt and two pieces of lining cloth.

Lay all the pieces together on top of each other: first felt, then two pieces of lining, then the second piece of felt. Pin them in position and then sew them together. (You can do this by hand, but it is better done on a sewing machine.) Along the open wrist-edge, turn the lining under and, with small hemming stitches, attach it to the felt all round the opening.

You can decorate the back of the glove with bits of different-coloured felt, sewing the pieces on to the glove with button-hole stitch or gluing them on.

Sew a loop or a brass ring on to one corner of the glove, so that it can be hung up in the kitchen.

A first book

You could make a first book for a baby which is designed especially for him, showing the sort of things with which he is familiar. You need some heavy white card, some tape about 2·5 centimetres (1 inch) wide and pictures cut from magazines. Decide the size of your book (20 centimetres [8 inches] is a good size) and cut out five pages. Cut your tape into pieces the same length as the side of your book. Glue the edges of two of the pieces of card, then lay them carefully side by side with a gap of 6 millimetres ($\frac{1}{4}$ inch) between them; keeping them in this position, attach them together by fixing a piece of tape over them. Stick the other pieces of card together in the same way until you have made a folding 'book'.

Now decorate your pages with your cut-out pictures and either letters or numbers, trying to make them as appropriate as possible; for instance, if the child has two sisters, use two girls to illustrate the number 'two'; if there are four trees in the garden, then use trees to illustrate 'four'.

A chest of drawers

You can make a tiny chest of drawers with matchboxes for someone's desk or dressing table or for a brother or sister who has a collection like stamps or coins.

Collect six empty matchboxes. Fix them firmly together with glue and stick a covering of adhesive plastic right round the outside and across the back. Take out each sliding 'drawer' and put a paper clip (the sort with two spikes and a head) as a handle.

You can, of course, make a chest of drawers as large as you wish by using more matchboxes, or you could use the larger household matchboxes to make a bigger chest of drawers, suitable for jewellery.

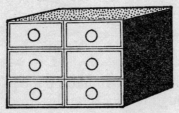

Decorated matchboxes

Stick coloured pictures on to ordinary or large matchboxes, making sure you don't stick anything over the striking side. Stick plain card over the matchbox and write the name of the person you give it to on the card.

A memo pad

You will need a piece of heavy card and a pad of paper which you can buy in a stationery shop (sometimes with 'Messages' or 'Don't Forget' printed on each sheet), a small pencil and some string.

Paint the heavy card or cover it with a piece of plain or patterned coloured paper or self-adhesive plastic. Punch two holes at the top about 5 centimetres (2 inches) apart and 1 centimetre ($\frac{1}{2}$ inch) down. Write or paint 'Messages' or 'Don't Forget' on the card below these holes if you have used a plain pad of paper. Paste the pad of paper firmly on to the card.

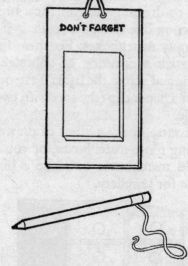

Make a narrow groove round the top of the pencil and tie the string round the pencil in this groove.

To make the string hold more firmly, stick a piece of coloured Sellotape round the pencil. Stick the other end of the string on to the card, on the right of the pad for a right-handed person or the left for a left-handed person.

Cut a picture from an old card and stick this firmly over the end of the string where it is stuck on to the card.

Tie another piece of string through the two holes at the top of the card; this is used for hanging up the memo pad.

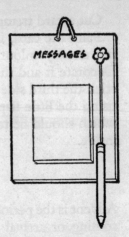

Bookmarks

The simplest bookmark can be made with a strip of light-coloured cardboard with pieces of paper or pictures stuck to it, like this:

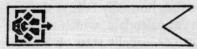

You can make a bookmark with a piece of grosgrain or corded ribbon about 23 centimetres (9 inches) long. Cut a triangle out of each end to stop the ribbon edge from un-ravelling. Stick a picture on to one end with glue.

Felt is also good for bookmarks and it doesn't fray. Cut a strip 4 by 23 centimetres ($1\frac{1}{2}$ by 9 inches) with either square or pointed ends. Decorate one end with embroidery or a pattern made with little pieces of coloured felt, which can be stuck or sewn on.

Another sort of bookmark can be made in the form of a corner, which is put over the corner of a page, like this:

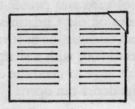

Cut a card triangle like this:
Paint the card, if it is
not already coloured.
Decorate it and then
stick the third side down,
using the little flap,
which should be tucked
inside.

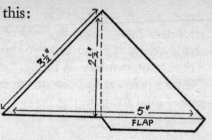

Advent calendars

Advent is the period leading up to Christmas. Advent means coming or arrival and this period is so named because it leads up to the coming of Christ on Christmas Day. The actual church season includes the four Sundays before Christmas, so that Advent Sunday, which marks the beginning of this period, normally falls at the end of November. However, Advent calendars, which mark off the days leading up to Christmas, usually start on 1 December. The idea is that each evening during December you open up another 'door' in the calendar to reveal a picture until finally, on Christmas Eve, you open the last one and the next day is Christmas Day. An Advent calendar is really a diary of your anticipation of the event to come! We have had great fun making our own, with the children taking it in turns to open up the doors each day. So either make one for yourself or make one as a present for a child or family you know.

A very simple one

Take a large piece of card and twenty-four 'Christmassy' pictures (keep pictures off old Christmas cards one year to be used in the Advent calendar the next year). Draw twenty-four doors on the card and, with a sharply pointed pair of scissors so you won't have to bend the card too much, cut them out, so that the doors can open:

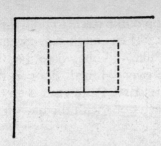

Behind each door paste a picture, and then shut the doors firmly again. Make two holes at the top of the piece of card and use this for a piece of ribbon or string with which the card can be hung up.

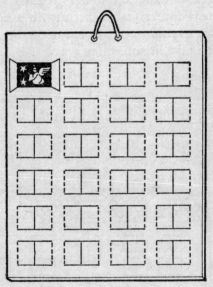

A clock face calendar

Take a big sheet of card and draw a big circle on it. You could draw round a large dinner plate or you could make a compass by tying a piece of string on to the end of a pencil, holding one end of the string firmly in the middle of the card and drawing a circle with the point of the pencil. Make two holes at the top of the circle to hold the string for hanging the calendar. Then mark off twenty-three 'doors' round the circle, like the ones described in the last item, and mark a large twenty-fourth door in the centre of the circle for Christmas Eve. Paste your pictures in behind the doors. Number each door with the day on which it is to be opened.

A do-it-yourself calendar

With this calendar, instead of opening up 'doors' you add a picture for each day, from a box which you have prepared in advance. Take a large piece of card, draw twenty-four spaces on it and write a number in each space. Collect together twenty-four suitable pictures in a box. Each day take it in turns to stick another picture on the calendar until it is completed on Christmas Eve.

An Advent house

Take a large piece of card and draw a house on it, with possibly a dog kennel and dovecot in the garden, a garage, perhaps both a front door and a side door and numerous windows. Make all the windows and doors open in the same

way as for the simple calendar on page 189. Paste pictures behind each door and window. On Christmas Eve the front door can be opened to show the final picture.

An Advent town

Paint twenty-four houses, shops and other buildings on your calendar with a picture behind each door.

An Advent wreath

In Germany some families make an Advent wreath of evergreen leaves, with four red candles fixed in it. This wreath stands on the table. The first candle is lit on the first Sunday after 26 November, which is Advent Sunday. The second and third candles are lit on the next two Sundays and the last one is lit on Christmas Eve.

It happened in November

1918 The Armistice between the Allied Powers and Germany was signed in the Forest of Compiègne in France on 11 November 1918, and the First World War came to an end after more than four years. We still remember the dead of both World Wars on Remembrance Sunday, the nearest Sunday to 11 November, and we buy poppies to aid the war victims and in memory of the poppies which grew on the soldiers' graves in Flanders.

November birthdays

Born between 23 October and 21 November, your zodiac sign is Scorpio – the scorpion. Scorpio people tend to be quiet and restrained, and to want privacy. They learn quickly, and easily understand abstract theories and ideas. But in spite of their calm appearance, they can often be bubbling with stored-up energy inside.

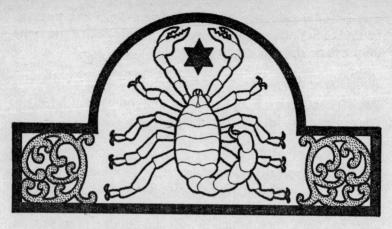

The birthstone for Scorpio is the topaz, which is a pale brown, blue, or colourless tone. The topaz is said to bring cheerfulness to its wearer, also long life, beauty and intelligence. It is also the symbol of friendship and faithfulness.

The lucky number for Scorpio is one; the lucky day Monday and the lucky colour white.

A riddle

In spring I look gay,
Decked in comely array,
In summer more clothing I wear;
When colder it grows,
I fling off my clothes,
And in winter quite naked appear.

A tree

No!

No sun – no moon!
  No morn – no noon –
No dawn – no dusk – no proper time of day –
  No sky – no earthy view –
  No distance looking blue –
No road – no street – no 't'other side the way' –
  No end to any Row –
No indication where the Crescents go –
  No top to any steeples –
No recognitions of familiar people –
  No courtesies for showing 'em –
  No knowing 'em! –
No travelling at all – no locomotion;
No inkling of the way – no notion –
  'No go' – by land or ocean –
No mail – no post –
No news from any foreign coast –
  No Park – no Ring – no afternoon gentility –
  No company – no nobility –
No warmth, no cheerfulness, no healthful ease,
  No comfortable feeling in any member –
No shade, no shine, no butterflies, no bees,
  No fruits, no flowers, no leaves, no birds –
  November!

Thomas Hood

NOVEMBER

My special days this month:

The weather this month:

The coldest day this month was:

The hottest day this month was:

In our park or garden I saw:

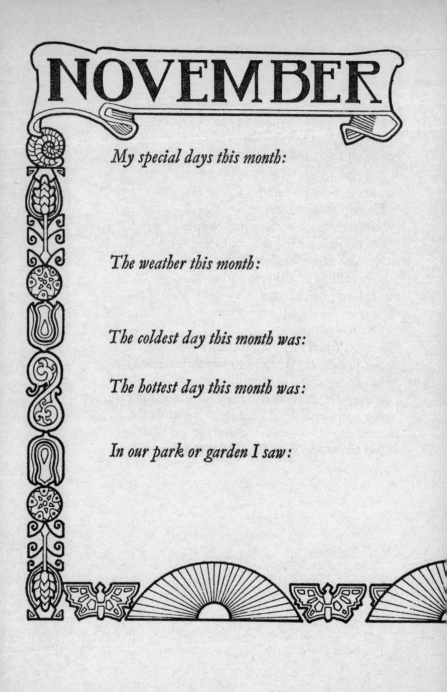

My Own Page

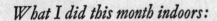

What I did this month indoors:

What I did this month outdoors:

The best/worst thing that happened this month:

Special events in the world this month:

DECEMBER

Chill December brings the sleet,
Blazing fires and Christmas treat.

The name of the month

December stands for the tenth month, which it used to be in the old calendar before January and February were added.

Festivals

St Nicholas's Day (6 December) is a European festival for the children. Little Dutch children put out their wooden shoes on the eve of St Nicholas and, if they have been good, there are sweets and cakes in the morning, but if they have been bad there is a switch to beat them with!

Christmas Day (25 December) is the day on which we celebrate the birth of Jesus Christ in the stable at Bethlehem.

Boxing Day (26 December). This is the day on which people used to go round collecting their Christmas 'box' for the work done by them during the year. Now we usually give

Christmas boxes to our postman, milkman and other people before Christmas and Boxing Day is a holiday for everybody.

Weather forecasts

A windy Christmas and calm Candlemas (2 February) are signs of a good year.

If New Year's Eve night-wind doth blow *south*
It betokens warmth and growth;
If *west*, much milk and fish in the sea;
If *north*, much storms and cold there will be;
If *east*, the trees will bear much fruit;
If *north-east*, flee it man and brute.

The last 'white Christmas', when snow fell on Christmas Day, was in 1956. How many years do you think it will be until the next one?

Sunrise and sunset

The sun is not up now until eight o'clock and has set before four. On 22 December you have the longest night and shortest day of the year and from that time the days gradually begin to lengthen.

Nature notes

If there is any late ploughing going on near the coast, you may see hungry seagulls hovering behind the plough to swoop down and pick up anything the plough-shares may turn over. Have you noticed how bright the evergreens look in winter when their dull green does not contrast with the brighter green of the deciduous trees?

Things to do outdoors
Snow

It may snow this month, so have ready a piece of black card (or even better, a piece of black velvet) and a magnifying glass. If it snows, go out and catch some snow flakes on the black background and look at their six-pointed patterns through the magnifying glass.

Snow acts as a blanket for the earth. You can test this with a thermometer. Measure the temperature on the surface and then underneath the snow. Which is warmer?

The birds

Start feeding the birds at your bird table again, for with winter here they may not be finding it easy to get all the food they need in the gardens and hedgerows. Make sure there is always a little bowl of water for them and check each morning that it is not frozen over.

Things to do indoors
A Christmas crib

In our family the Christmas crib is put up on the hall mantelpiece during December with a night-light candle in a safe position beside it in a little dish of water. The children see it on their way to bed each night. We had first a plaster crib which I had had as a child and then a card-figure nativity scene which we made together. Here are some ideas about how to make one of your own.

You can make all the human and angel figures, except for that of baby Jesus, from the same basic pattern, only varying the sizes.

Draw a circle with a compass on plain or coloured paper or light-weight card. If you haven't got a compass, draw your circle round different-sized saucers and small plates. Fold the circle in half, then in quarters. Cut a circle out of the centre and then cut along the folds in the paper, so that you

have four pieces like this for the bodies. Form each body into a cone and glue it together at the back. If you use white paper, paint suitable clothing on to it. If you are using coloured paper, use different colours for different figures and use bits of white paper and other coloured paints to decorate the figure.

For the heads you will need plain wooden balls or balls made from papiermâché or Plasticine. Paint the features on to these faces. Fix the head on to the neck of the body cone.

For the arms you will need a piece of curved paper cut from one of the circles.

Check that the arms are the right length for the body when they are fixed at the back and round the sides of the figure, like this:

Then round off the ends for the hands. You can fix the arm piece on so that the arms point either up or down, like this:

You now have your basic figure ready to decorate. Decide who each figure is to be and give them suitable hair and features.

The hair can be made either from bits of wool or with paper. For paper hair, cut a strip of paper about 2·5 centimetres (1 inch) wide, fringe one side of it, then roll the strip tightly round a knitting needle so that it curls up. Glue the hair round the head. Beards can be made in the same way or from bits of combed-out cotton wool, which can be dipped in paint to colour. Make the features very simple: eyes painted on with black paint would be quite enough.

Now for the clothes. You can make a cloak by cutting one of the quarter-circles shorter and fixing it on over the arms of the figure. The cloaks can be quite long or very short, like shawls. You can make a broad-brimmed hat by cutting a circle of paper, folding it gently in half (so that it doesn't crease) and cutting a short line across it, then folding it in the opposite direction and cutting another line. Fold

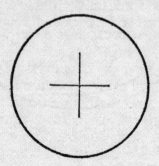

the flaps thus cut upwards. Take a thin strip of paper, about 1 centimetre ($\frac{1}{2}$ inch) wide and glue it round, fixed on to the flaps of the brim.

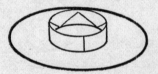

A woman's headdress can be made like a headscarf from a small piece of soft cloth.

An apron can be made by cutting out a piece of paper with two ties, like this:

and pasting it round the waist of the figure.

Mary should have a blue dress and cloak and a white headdress.

Joseph can have a cloak and brimmed hat and can carry a straw as a staff.

The shepherds can be dressed much like Joseph, though possibly in duller colours. You could turn up the brims on their hats and they could also carry staves.

The innkeeper can also be dressed like Joseph, though possibly with a shorter cloak and no hat or staff.

The innkeeper's wife could have an apron and a coloured headscarf.

The wise men will be much more grandly dressed than the others. Use colourful paper for their bodies and cloaks and paint or glue patterns and glitter on to their clothes. Cut crowns from strips of gilt or silver paper and glue them round their heads on to the back. Scraps of coloured paper can be jewels in their crowns. You can give them gifts to carry in their hands, which are glued together to hold them.

The angel can have a short white cloak, but fixed at the back. Wings made from gold or silver paper can be fixed over this. Wings can be made in this shape:

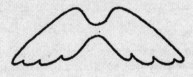

Stick a circle of stiff gilt paper at the back of the angel's head for a halo.

Animals (sheep, an ox, a donkey) can be made from folded card. Cut out the shape through both pieces, so that the animal can stand on four legs. Colour their bodies and mark in their eyes. You could cover the sheep with cotton wool.

Baby Jesus is made from a small square of paper which is formed into a tube, with a small round ball of wood or Plasticine stuck on for the head. His halo, a small circle of gilt paper, is stuck on to the back of the head. His arms are made and fixed on in the same way as those of the larger figures. He can be placed in a manger made from a little box. Prop it up at the back, so that you can see the baby inside. Fill the box with little pieces of cotton wool or straw for the baby to lie on.

For the *stable* use a smallish cardboard box (like a children's shoe box*) which you can paint. Fix a folded piece of brown or straw coloured corrugated paper on to the top as a roof. You will need a piece about half as wide again as the top of the box. Fold it in half lengthways. Put a line of fast-drying glue (like Bostik or Uhu) along the edge of the box and put the roof on top of it so that it just catches along the edge and leaves an 'eave' jutting out front and back. If you had some bits of straw you could stick these on to the roof.

Make a *star* from gold or silver paper and suspend it on a dark thread above the stable.

* Did you know that when you buy shoes in a shop you can always ask for the box and they will be pleased to give it to you.

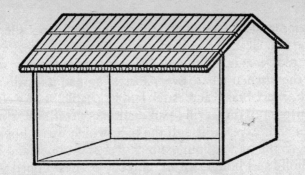

Place a piece of brown or green cloth on the shelf or table where the crib is to stand and put the stable, figures and star in position on it. You could add a few pieces of straw and some evergreen leaves to make it look more real.

You can use this sort of figure to make other groups, such as a group of carol-singing choir boys in red robes with

white collars (short cloaks fixed on back to front like the angel's) and holding hymn books in front of them with their hands.

Christmas decorations

'A few days before Christmas Tom Garland and Dan took a bill-hook and knife and went into the woods to cut branches of scarlet-berried holly. They tied them together with ropes and dragged them down over the fields, to the barn.

'Tom cut a bough of mistletoe from the ancient hollow hawthorn which leaned over the wall by the orchard, and thick clumps of dark-berried ivy from the walls.

'Indoors Mrs Garland and Susan and Becky polished and rubbed and cleaned the furniture and brasses, so that everything glowed and glittered. They decorated every room, from the kitchen where every lustre jug had its sprig in its mouth, every brass candlestick had its chaplet, every copper saucepan and preserving-pan had its wreath of shining berries and leaves, through the hall, which was a bower of green, to the two parlours, which were festooned and hung with holly and boughs of fir, and ivy berries dipped in red raddle, left over from sheep marking.

'Holly decked every picture and ornament. Sprays hung over the bacon and twisted round the hams and herb bunches. The clock carried a crown on his head, and every dish-cover had a little sprig. Susan kept an eye on the lonely, forgotten, humble things, the jelly moulds and colanders and nutmeg-graters, and made them happy with glossy leaves. Everything seemed to speak, to ask for its morsel of greenery, and she tried to leave out nothing.'

The Country Child, Alison Uttley

Christmas decorations to make

Paper chains

The simplest sort of paper chains are very easy to make. You will need some coloured paper (the pages of a coloured magazine are effective and both tissue and crêpe paper are good, but any coloured paper will do so long as it is not too heavy); scissors and glue. Mark the paper into strips and then cut them out. If you want a tree decoration, your strips should be not more than 1 centimetre ($\frac{1}{2}$ inch) wide and 7 centimetres (3 inches) long; if you want to decorate the room, they can be 2·5 centimetres (1 inch) wide and 15 centimetres (6 inches) long.

Make the strips into chains of one, by gluing one end and bringing the other end over to stick to it. Pass the next strip through the first link before gluing it and go on like this

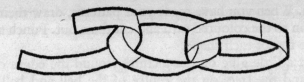

until your chain is as long as you want. Remember that you want it to hang in loops like this, so do make it long enough.

A *picture chain*

You will need some different-coloured card or thick paper, a length of narrow ribbon and a tube of glitter. You will also need stiff card for patterns (this is where the backs of old Christmas cards can be useful, *see* page 16). Make patterns like these from which you can trace pictures for your

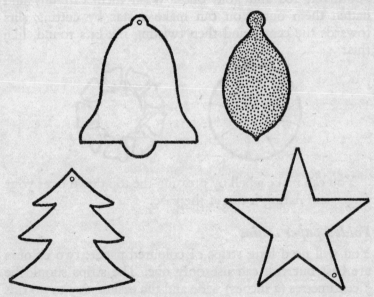

chain. When you have made your patterns, draw their outline on to the coloured card and cut them out. Punch a hole at the top of each shape.

Put a little glue on the pictures (round the edges of the star and the tree, on the centre of the bell and ball) and scatter glitter on the glue. Let it dry, then shake off any extra glitter on to a sheet of paper so that you can use it again. Turn the shapes over and put glitter on the other side.

Now string your pictures on to the ribbon, alternating the colours and keeping them about 5 centimetres (2 inches) or more away from each other. You can use a picture chain with small shapes for the tree, or make one with larger shapes to decorate the room.

Tree decorations from milk bottle tops

Collect together a number of milk-bottle tops, trying to get silver, red and gold ones. Wash them carefully and flatten them out. You can make a star by cutting slits towards the centre and then twisting the bits round, like this:

You can make a bell by pressing the top down over your finger and flaring it out at the base.

Folded paper chains

You will need long strips of coloured paper; two colours are best but you can use only one. The strips should be 5 centimetres (2 inches) wide and the easiest way to do this is to take a packet of crêpe paper and cut straight across it

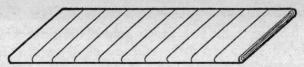

in 5-centimetre (2-inch) slices without unfolding the packet, as shown above.

Now, take the end of one strip and glue it at right angles to the end of another strip, like this:

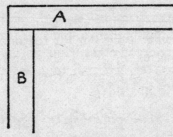

Fold one strip over the other, then the second over the first, the first over the second again, and so on until you have used the whole strip. Then you can either add more strips by gluing them on to the end of the last two and continuing the 'weaving' or you can glue the ends of your strips together and open them out into a chain. Remember to make it long enough to hang in loops, as shown on page 205.

Put out more flags

Make coloured flags from paper or cloth. Fix them on to a string and hang them across the room.

A Christmas star

This represents the star which guided the three kings to Bethlehem. You can make different sized stars in foil or coloured paper to use as Christmas-tree decorations, to decorate parcels or, a very large one, to hang on your front door. My niece gave me a shiny green one a few years ago and it decorates our front door every year.

You will need foil or coloured paper – tissue paper will do. Cut a strip four times as long as it is wide. Your star will be twice as wide across as the width of your strip, so if you want a big star for the door, make a strip 60 by 15 centimetres (24 by 6 inches) and you will get a star 30 centimetres (12 inches) across. Fold it as you do to make a paper fan, like this:

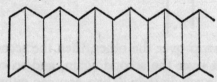

Cut points at one end of the folded strip and, if you want patterns on your star, cut some shapes on the folded edges.

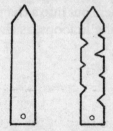

With a needle thread a thin bit of twine through the uncut edge of the folded strip. Open out the strip like a fan and tighten the twine as you do so, pulling the fan round into a circle. Stick the two edges of the strip together to hold it in shape. If you want to keep the star from year to year, as I do mine, don't fix it permanently; use Sellotape, and then you can fold it back flat again.

You can make a similar star in another way. Go through the stages which bring you to a folded strip, then trim off *both* ends. Fold this strip at the centre, like this:

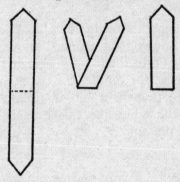

Sew firmly through this fold.

Gum or sew the two centre sides of the strip together and then open out the strip like a fan until it forms a full circle. Stick the other sides of the strip together.

A holly wreath for the front door or table

You will need some medium-weight wire or a narrow strip of chicken wire and a variety of evergreen leaves and berries. If you are using wire, twist it round on itself, so that there are slits between each strand. If you use chicken wire wrap it round into a circle and cover it with 'bandages' of crêpe paper wound round and round but leaving spaces for the sprigs of evergreen.

Fix a string on to the wire base and then decorate the wire base thickly with your evergreen leaves. Hang the finished wreath on your front door. You can use a wreath like this as a table decoration, but place it on a mat so the wire won't scratch the table.

A log for the table

Find a small log with an interesting surface and rough bark. Split it in half, like this:

Decorate the log with touches of white paint or by gluing parts of it and sticking on artificial snow and fuzzed-up cotton wool. Fix on to the log a Plasticine strip which can be used as the base for candles, fir cones, holly and other evergreen leaves, perhaps a bit of ribbon and tinsel. A decoration for the table like this can also make a very good Christmas present.

Trees to make

Get a flower pot, fill it with plaster and put a straight, tall stick into it for the trunk of the tree. Tie a block of 'Oasis' (material used for flower arranging, available from florists) to the top. Stick pieces of holly, ivy, fir and other evergreens into it to make a tree.

A CHRISTMAS BRANCH TREE

Fix a branch into a flower pot filled with earth or, to make it steadier, with plaster. Tip the branch with white paint and bits of 'cotton wool snow'. Add some green paper leaves. Hang some glass Christmas balls or silver stars from it. Make some paper birds to sit on the branches.

A CRACKER TREE

Fix some pieces of wire into a flower pot full of earth or plaster.

Then put the crackers on the 'branches' of your cracker tree, so that the wire goes through the middle of the crackers like this:

The only disadvantage with this idea as a decoration is that the branches return to bare wires when you remove the crackers!

ADAM'S TREE

I call this tree after my son, who made the first one I saw like this (following someone else's design, admittedly). You can make it as a Christmas tree or as an Easter tree with light-green 'leaves' and spring 'flowers' or you can make it as a Harvest tree with 'apples', when it could best be called Adam's tree!

Take four sheets of newspaper and glue them together one on top of another, with flour-and-water paste, so that you have paper four layers thick. Cut your paper so that it forms a square. Then roll it up to form a cone: do this by keeping one end pointed and letting the other spread more

loosely to form the base. Glue into position and trim the base level so that it will stand firmly. Leave it to dry. Stick green crêpe paper over the cone, using Sellotape to join the seams. Now cut out a large number of green tissue-paper squares or circles about 6 centimetres ($2\frac{1}{2}$ inches) across. Twist these into flowers by crushing them together at the centre, so that they look like this:

Now stick these flower shapes all over the tree cone as close together as you can until it is covered. If you are making an Easter tree, use some white, pink and yellow flowers amongst the green; and if you are making a Harvest tree stick small red flowers among the green to represent apples.

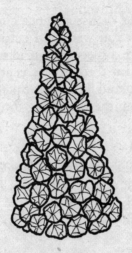

Your tree can stand on a table by itself, or you could give it a trunk by putting a straight, stout stick into a pot full of plaster and simply placing the cone over it, so that the tree would look like the drawing opposite.

You could, of course, make little trees of any size by using smaller cones and smaller pieces of tissue paper for the 'leaves'. You could use these trees for table decorations or stand them in painted yoghurt pots and give them as Christmas presents.

More hanging decorations

Here are some ideas for more complicated decorations to use for the Christmas tree or, if you make them large enough, for room decorations.

PAPER BALLS

Cut a large number of tissue-paper circles by folding the paper into the size you want and cutting through several layers at once. Take a piece of thread with a good knot at one end and thread it through the centre of all the pieces. Pull the thread tight and fluff out the paper to make the ball. Hang your ball from the remaining thread.

CUT-OUT SHAPES

Make a symmetrical shape like a triangle, square or circle – a triangle is the best one to start with. Fold it in half, then fold it back again the other way on the same fold line. Cut across the fold as shown in the picture. Open it out again,

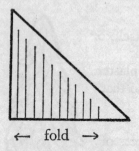

← fold →

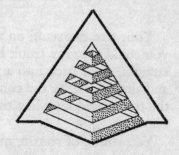

then pull out the cut pieces in opposite directions. It makes it easier to do this if you thread a pencil through first to divide them and pull them apart. Put a thread through the top to hang the shapes with. The triangle and square could be used to make a card if they were the right size, because they will stand up.

Wrapping presents and decorating parcels

The wrapping paper you can buy in the shops always seems to me to be very expensive, except for coloured tissue paper, so I suggest this and white kitchen paper as the best sort for you to use. At Christmas time we collect together all the nicest pieces of paper which we get on our presents, fold or roll them away carefully and bring them out again next year to use to send presents to other people! The big piece that someone gave you last year will usually be quite good enough to wrap a smaller present with no signs that it has been used before.

First of all let's look at ways of wrapping various basic shapes. Later we'll look at ways of decorating the parcels you have made.

Square or rectangular parcels

Lay the parcel on the paper and cut the paper so that it is not too long at the sides of the parcel.

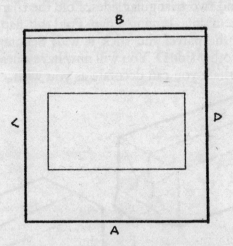

Fold side B down 1 centimetre ($\frac{1}{2}$ inch) at the edge, to make a smooth edge. Wrap side A over the top of the parcel. Then wrap side B over this. Fold the top part of side C

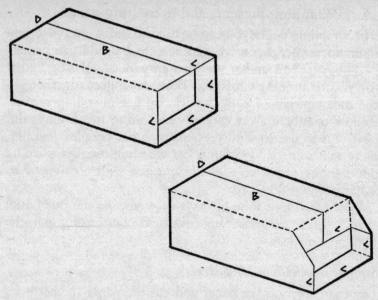

downwards against the edge of the parcel, so that you have one edge and two triangular sides. Fold the triangular sides towards the middle, leaving a flap. Fold this flap up against the end of the parcel and stick it with Sellotape. Do the same at the other side D. You will now have a neat rectangular parcel which you can decorate as you wish.

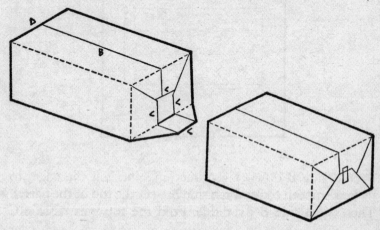

A cylinder or roll

There are three ways to wrap this sort of parcel. But you start all three in the same way. Lay the parcel on its side on the paper and roll the paper round it. You may find it easier now if you fix the edge down with glue or Sellotape.

The three ways are as follows:

1. Fold the top half of one end down as you do for a square parcel. Make a second fold with half the remaining paper, a third fold with the other half, and then fold down and fix the triangular corner which remains. Do the other end in the same way.

2. Fold and fix one end as you did for 1. At the other end, where there should be about twice as much paper, pull the paper together as close to the top of the cylinder as possible. Put a piece of Sellotape or a rubber band round the paper as near the parcel as possible and fluff out the top paper. You could fringe this paper with scissors.

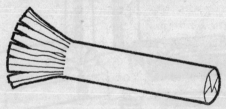

3. Make a cracker shape by pulling in the paper at both ends of the cylinder with Sellotape or rubber bands, and fluffing out or fringing the ends.

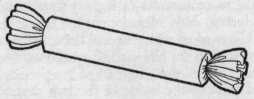

Flat parcels

When you are wrapping something like a book or a calendar, lay the present on the centre of the paper and fold over both sides. Then make triangular folds at the corners of the open ends and bring the flap thus made down on to the parcel. Sellotape it in position.

This method is also suitable for things like scarves, sweaters and other soft articles and can be used to wrap many irregular-shaped parcels. When you want to conceal the shape of your present (e.g. a doll or a toy train) you may find it easier to wrap it first in a layer of corrugated paper before putting on the outer wrapping.

Decorating parcels

You can tie your parcel with ribbon in a number of different ways. Here are a few suggestions for you to try out.

Wrap your parcel with newspaper sealed with red sealing wax and tied with red ribbon. Decorate the parcel with red paint.

Make a box

Take a piece of card of suitable size. Overleaf we show a flattish box 10 centimetres (4 inches) square and 5 centimetres (2 inches) deep. Measure out the box as shown; cut away the bits marked with diagonal lines; make cuts where shown and fold in the bits marked with dots. Score all the other lines. Fold all the bits marked A upwards and stick the dotted sides to the inside of the two nearest A sides. Then fold up B and fix in the two other dotted sides. C is the lid of the box and the remaining dotted bit is the flap which is slotted in to hold the lid down:

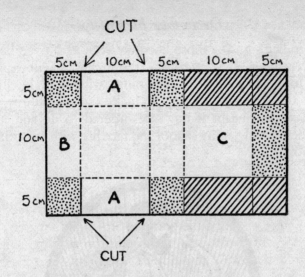

It happened in December

1791 The composer Mozart died on 5 December.

1903 Orville Wright flew the first aeroplane in America on 17 December.

1906 On 24 December the world's first ever advertised broadcast went out over the air in America.

1911 The Norwegian explorer, Amundsen, reached the South Pole on 16 December.

December birthdays

The zodiac sign for those born between 22 November and 21 December is Sagittarius – the archer. Sagittarians are said to be friendly and outgoing, witty and intelligent. They are honest, but happy-go-lucky and spendthrift. They can become defiant if they are ordered to do something, but they usually enjoy school and face life with an optimistic outlook.

The birthstone for Sagittarius is the turquoise; it gets its name from Turkey, whence it was first introduced to Europe. It is a greeny-blue stone, and it is said to bring prosperity, success and good fortune to its wearer.

Sagittarians' lucky colour is red, their lucky number is 2 and their lucky day is Sunday.

Christmas in a village

Each house is swept the day before,
And windows stuck with evergreens;
The snow is besomed from the door,
And comfort crowns the cottage scenes.
Gilt holly with its thorny pricks
And yew and box with berries small
These deck the unused candle sticks,
And pictures hanging by the wall.

John Clare

Now thrice welcome Christmas,
Which brings us good cheer,
Minced pies and plum porridge,
Good ale and strong beer;
With pig, goose and capon,
The best that may be,
So well doth the weather
And our stomachs agree.

From *Poor Robin's Almanac*, 1695

And now we are round to New Year's Eve (31 December)
and New Year's Day, and the first footing again.

DECEMBER

My special days this month:

The weather this month:

The coldest day this month was:

The hottest day this month was:

In our park or garden I saw:

My Own Page

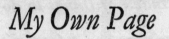

What I did this month indoors:

What I did this month outdoors:

The best/worst thing that happened this month:

Special events in the world this month:

Index of things to do

Indoors

Bonfire Night: food, 167–8, 177; invitations, 158; masks, 159–61

Decorating: Christmas parcels, 218; Easter eggs, 66–7; matchboxes, 185–6

Games to play: Donna's Patience, 36–8; Nine Men's Morris, 20–1

Giving a party: crackers, 80; food, 83–7; games, 87; invitations, 79; napkin rings, 81; paper cups and hats, 81–2; table decorations, 80

Hallowe'en: fancy dress, 162–5; food, 167–8; games, 165–7; invitations ,159; Jack o'lantern, 161–2; masks, 159–61

Planting bulbs, 149–50

Things to make: Advent wreath, 191; baby's first book, 184–5; bath-salts jar, 117; birthday cards, 103–5; bookmarks, 187–8; calendars, 17–20, 188–91; Christmas cards, 177–81; Christmas crib, 198–203; Christmas decorations, 203–14; Christmas presents, 182–8; cuff links ,117–18; Easter biscuits, 69; Easter cards, 52–3; Easter presents, 70–71; Father's Day presents, 100–102; flower buttonhole, 100; football scarf, 147–8; get well cards, 34–5; harvest decorations, 144–7; matchbox chest of drawers, 185; memo pad, 186–7; Mothering Sunday presents, 50–1; notice board, 135; oven glove, 183–4; parkins, 177; pencil holder, 119–20; pomander, 182–3; potato-cut cards, 103–4; presents for teacher, 115–20; pressed-flower pictures, 102–3; rain gauge, 133–4; screwdriver holder, 101–2; seed collage, 148–9; shortbread biscuits, 118–19; Shrove Tuesday pancakes, 49; spray-paint pictures, 104–5; spring-flower pictures, 50–52; sugar Easter eggs, 67–8; summer holiday diary, 120–21; sweets, 33–4; thank you cards, 115–17; toothpaste holder, 102; Valentine cards, 32–3; wax pictures, 105; wormery, 132–3; your own barometer, 50

Using old Christmas cards, 16–17

Watching seeds grow, 53–4

Wrapping Christmas presents, 215–18

Outdoors

Burying a 'time treasure', 144

Collecting: autumn leaves, 156–7; conkers, 157; shells and stones, 113–14; tadpoles, 46–7

Experimenting with buds, 30–31

Feeding the birds, 13–15, 198

Games to play: boule, 128; conker base, 143; fives, 128–9; Malayan football, 97–8; on the beach, 113–14; plate tennis, 97; shadow tag, 97

Holiday visits, 131–2

Identifying: birds, 15; grasses, 97; mushrooms, 79

Keeping a wind record, 64–5

Looking at: snowflakes, 198; the Milky Way, 144

Observing the country code, 98–9

Picnicking, 94–9

Recognizing trees in winter, 176–7

Remembering the fireworks code, 176

Taking a mystery tour, 46

Things to make: bird pudding, 30; bird table, 13–15; flower and leaf chains, 129–30; snowman, 15–16; sun clock, 78; wild-flower collection, 130–1

Watching: spiders, 114–15; meteors, 128

224